The
Ferret
Handbook

Gerry Bucsis and Barbara Somerville

With Full-Color Photographs by the Authors

Dedication

This book is dedicated to Patch and Gabby—two fun-filled furballs!

Photo Credits

Behling & Johnson provided photos on front cover left, top middle, and bottom right, inside front cover, and page viii. Photos on pages 12, 23, 59, 90, 99, 107, 120, 121, 164, and 165 courtesy of Marshall Pet Products. Photos on pages 20, 21, 26, 27, 66, 76, 91, and 104 courtesy of "Super Pet" Pets International, Ltd. Ferret treats on pages 30 and 32 courtesy of Eight In One Pet Products, Inc. Harnesses and leashes on pages 107 and 156 courtesy of Rolf C. Hagen, Inc. Super Chew Toy on page 41 and hat on page 36 courtesy of Marshall Pet Products. Cages on pages 21 and 74 by Midwest Homes for pets. Smart Crock on page 25 by Pearce Plastics. Giant Roll-a-Nest on pages 5 and 76, treat ball on pages 6 and 98, bowl on page 31, litter boxes on pages 65 and 66, and cage clips on page 75 courtesy of "Super Pet" Pets International, Ltd.

All inquiries should be addressed to:
Barron's Educational Series, Inc.
250 Wireless Boulevard
Hauppauge, New York 11788
http://www.barronseduc.com

ISBN-13: 978-0-7641-1323-9
ISBN-10: 0-7641-1323-2

Library of Congress Catalog Card No. 00-57148

Library of Congress Cataloging-in-Publication Data
Bucsis, Gerry.
      The ferret handbook / Gerry Bucsis and Barbara
Somerville; with photos by the authors.
      p.   cm.
Includes bibliographical references (p.).
ISBN 0-7641-1323-2
      1. Ferrets as pets. I. Somerville, Barbara II. Title.
SF459.F47 B83   2001
636.9'76628—dc21
                                                  00-57148

Printed in China
19 18 17 16 15 14 13 12

Acknowledgments

Special thanks to:
• our families for their support, understanding, and encouragement
• our editor, Anna Damaskos, who always has time for us no matter how busy she gets
• to our friends, Janie, Mary, and Lindsay for allowing us to photograph their ferrets
• Robin Leous, for her kindness and cooperation
• Diane Pawelko, for unfailing help and support
• Dr. John Valsamis, DVM, for expert advice and ferret care
• the following companies for their help and cooperation:
   Absorption Corporation: Ampro Industries; The Barnaby Company; Canbrands International, Ltd.; Contech Electronics, Inc.; Eight In One Pet Products, Inc.; Fangman Specialties, Inc.; Flukers Ferret Food; Gentle Touch Products; Grannick's Bitter Apple Company; Green Pet Products; Rolf C. Hagen, Inc.; Hyper-Fur Products; Kaytee Products, Inc.; Lambert Kay; L/M Animal Farms; Marshall Pet Products, Inc.; Midwest Homes for Pets; Mountain Meadows Products, Inc.; Nature's Earth Products, Inc.; Nu-Gro Corporation; Oxyfresh Worldwide, Inc.; Paulmac's Pet Store, St. Catharine's ON (Thanks again, Joan and Roy!); Performance Foods, Inc.; PetSmart, St. Catharine's ON; Pet Valu, Fonthill, ON (Thanks, Sarah and Ron!); P.J. Murphy Forest Products Corp.; Purina Mills, Inc.; Sheppard and Greene; Sun Seed Co., Inc.; "Super Pet" Pets International, Ltd.; Tomlyn Products; WAL-MART Photo Finishing team, Welland, ON.

Note of Warning

This book deals with the keeping and training of ferrets as pets. In working with these animals, you may occasionally sustain scratches or bites. Administer first aid immediately, and seek medical attention if necessary.

Ferrets must be watched carefully during the necessary and regular exercise periods in the house. To avoid life-threatening accidents, be particularly careful that your pet does not gnaw on rubber, foam, latex, sponge, or electric cords.

If your ferret shows any sign of illness, be sure to visit your veterinarian.

Contents

VOID

Chapter One

Is a Ferret the Right Pet for You?

The Ferret— a Popular Pet

Although they haven't caught up to cats and dogs yet, ferrets are definitely gaining points in the pet popularity polls. In fact, they're the third most popular companion pet in North America. And no wonder! Have you ever seen a cage full of baby ferrets (kits)? They have all the instant appeal of puppies and kittens. They're cute. They're cuddly. They're energetic and entertaining. In other words, those little kits are pretty darn irresistible. And, adult ferrets are just as playful—they don't wind down as they grow up.

But please, don't let the cuteness factor influence your judgment. Don't ever buy any kind of pet without doing your homework first.

Ferrets need a good-sized cage. Can you afford one?

Do Your Homework First

Ferrets are unique pets . . . they're not like kittens or puppies, cats or dogs. Their behavior, their needs, and their care requirements are different. It's up to you to find out what's involved in caring for a ferret day after day after day. For example, how do ferrets behave in the home? Can they be litter-trained? How much playtime do they need? Can they roam free, or do they need to be caged?

Do you know the answers to these questions? So many people buy pets without thinking much about what they're getting into. Don't be one of them. Preplan your pet purchase carefully. Read as many books as you can. Speak to other ferret owners. Surf the Net. And visit pet shops or breeders to observe ferrets firsthand. Know what you're taking on *before* you bring one home.

Kits are cute and cuddly—but find out the facts before bringing one home.

Focus On the Future

Ferrets live from five to seven years—and some live even longer. Can you commit to taking care of a ferret for this long? It's cruel to bring Bandit home and *then* decide that he's not the pet for you. It's unkind to keep Fresca for a year and then have to find a new home for her because you're going off to university or because you're moving to a "no pets" apartment. Think how the poor ferret would feel being palmed off and deserted by the only family she's ever known.

So look beyond the moment . . . consider your future plans very carefully before forking out for a ferret. Buying a pet is a huge commitment—or it should be. You have to think of a pet purchase as a new family member coming into the house. Pets are NOT disposable.

Does a Ferret Fit Your Lifestyle?

If you think ferrets are caged pets like hamsters or gerbils—think again. They're companion pets like cats and dogs. You wouldn't keep a Chihuahua or a Calico cooped up in a cage around the clock, would you? Why, then, would you keep a ferret caged all day? To be happy and well-adjusted, your buddy needs at least three to four hours of playtime every day. She needs to run, romp, sniff, snoop, jump, and generally ferret around. Otherwise, she'll suffer from depression and behavior problems. So take a good look at your lifestyle. Do you have enough hours on your hands to give a ferret the attention she needs and deserves? Don't bring a fuzzy home unless you have time for one.

Fortunately, ferrets are real sleepyheads. They snooze anywhere from 14 to 16 hours per day, sometimes even more, so they make great pets for working people. Are you slaving away at an office eight hours per day? Not a problem. Your ferret can adjust her schedule so she's sleeping when you're at work and raring to go when you return. Just make sure that you've got enough get-up-and-go to play with your pal before work and again when you get home. Exercise, play, and companionship are three basic ferret needs. If you can't meet those needs, better forgo a ferret altogether and pick a different pet.

Another lifestyle issue to consider is travel. Do you find yourself racking up the miles either for business or pleasure? If you're on the go a lot, what's going to happen to your ferret? Although many ferrets are good travelers (see Chapter 12), they can't go everywhere with everybody. For example, ferrets are banned in certain places and require licenses in others. They're also prone to heatstroke, and heatstroke can be life threatening to ferrets. Leaving them at home can be a headache, too— boarding a ferret isn't always as easy as boarding a cat or a dog. So, if you're a tireless traveler, take a good look at what your travels involve and figure whether or not a ferret will fit into your plans.

Can You Afford a Ferret?

Devoted pet owners tend not to count costs. They regard every penny spent on their pal as a penny well spent. However, what if costs outrun cash? Then there are tough decisions to be made. That's why it's important to be realistic about budgeting before you bring a pet home. Add up the total cost of pet ownership. Make sure that the pet you've set your heart on is also the one that sits well with your budget.

Here's what you need to take into account when a ferret's your pet of choice. For starters, there's the initial purchase price. This could vary significantly depending on where you buy the ferret, whether she is already spayed and/or descented, and whether rare colors or championship bloodlines are involved.

Ferrets sleep a lot—they make good pets for busy families.

Then there's the cost of equipment. The cage is the main item and the main expense. Add in bowls, litter boxes, nail clippers, brush, harness, and leash. As well as these one-time outlays, there are ongoing month-to-month expenses such as food, litter, shampoo, conditioners, and treats. Fortunately, where ferrets are concerned, these recurring costs are very reasonable.

Last but not least, you'll need to factor in the cost of veterinary care. Veterinary expenses come in two forms. First there's the cost of ongoing preventative care. This includes annual checkups, immunizations for canine distemper and rabies, hairball medicine, heartworm prevention medication, flea and tick programs, and yearly diagnostic tests for older ferrets. A call to your local animal clinic will give you a handle on these costs.

Second—and the real unknown—is the size of the vet bills you'll have to foot if your ferret develops medical problems. Like all pets, ferrets can get sick. Medical intervention can be expensive and is something that needs to be planned for. A small amount put aside every paycheck into a cookie jar can go a long way to ease the ouch.

Are You Allergy Prone?

Allergies to pets are nothing to sneeze at. So if you suffer from allergies, do yourself a favor. Before buying a ferret, find out if you can tolerate a furball or if she'll be one more item on your allergy list. First, consult your doctor and ask for his or her advice. Has your doctor given you the OK to consider a pet? Then the next step is to get up close and personal to a ferret. Visit a pet shop, shelter, breeder, or ferret owner and handle some ferrets. Five minutes handling won't do—stay for a good long time. One visit won't do, either—make it three or four. No reactions? Then chances are that a ferret's a pet possibility for you.

Are your eyes watering? Are you itching? Have you developed a rash? Are you short of breath? Are you wheezing or coughing? Better play it safe and bypass the ferrets. Otherwise, your health could be at risk, and the little ferret's future could be at risk, too. Where's she going to end up if you buy her and your allergic reactions are so bothersome that you can't keep her?

Are There Young Children in the House? (Or Going to Be?)

Many veterinarians don't recommend a ferret as a pet for children under the age of ten. Why? Young children are not always gentle with animals. Intentional mishandling is not usually the problem here—just the opposite, in fact. It's an excess of affection that sometimes has kids squeezing their pets and dragging them around like stuffed toys. But wiggly kits don't enjoy being snuggled like stuffed teddies—they won't put up with being restrained. And ferrets of any age won't stand having their ears pulled, their tails yanked, their eyes poked, or their ribs squeezed. The child could be bitten or scratched, the ferret could be dropped and injured—everyone will end up unhappy.

So if there are young children in the house, it's probably best to postpone your ferret purchase for a while. This way there'll be no chance of child or pet being hurt. You'll also make things easy on yourself—you won't have a ferret and a child going through the terrible two's together.

Can You Ferret Proof Your Home?

Ferrets are curious critters. As soon as you open that cage door— *whoosh!*—they're off and running, sticking their noses into every hole and corner, looking for mischief. But in the average home, there are too many accidents waiting to happen to free-roaming ferrets. So you can't just bring a ferret home and let it start running loose in the house— you need to ferret proof first. What is ferret proofing? It's making the play space safe *for* your ferret and safe *from* your ferret. Read Chapter 6 to find out what's involved in ferret proofing. Then determine whether or not you're prepared to take the time and trouble. Remember, ferrets are companion pets and need lots of out-of-the-cage playtime. If you can't guarantee your ferret's safety everywhere in the house, you'll need to provide at least one ferret-proofed room for fun and frolics.

Check the Law and Check with the Landlord

Some states, cities, and towns have declared themselves "Ferret Free Zones" (FFZ's). In these places,

The great investigator.

ferrets are often classified as exotic pets, or misclassified as wild animals, and banned by law. Laws change, however, so it's not possible to give an accurate, up-to-date list of FFZ's. Because ferrets can be confiscated or even put to death in the areas where they're banned, it's up to you to make sure ferrets are legal where you live before you buy one. It's also your responsibility to find out about ferret fees and/or licenses. These are still mandatory in some towns and states. In fact, in some states, a license is required even if you're just ferrying your fuzzy through that state on the way to somewhere else.

If you don't own your own home, check your rental or lease agreement before making any pet purchase. Some agreements ban pets altogether. Others allow only certain types of pets—a fish may be fine, but a ferret may be forbidden. And if you know you're going to be moving, think twice before adopting a furball. The pet that's welcome at your present apartment could be outlawed at your next address.

Ferret Fragrance

Ugh! Many people are under the impression that all ferrets smell like

A neutered or spayed ferret makes the best house pet.

skunks. Fortunately, this doesn't have to be the case. Here are the facts.

Ferrets in their natural, non-neutered state do have a very pronounced body odor. Have you ever been around a whole male when he comes into season? Wow! What a stink! And unspayed females can be a noseful, too. What's causing the smell? It's those sex hormones working hard to attract a mate. So to stop the smell, you need to stop the hormone production. How's this to be done? Fixing your ferret's the answer because when neutering or spaying is taken care of, the bulk of ferret B.O. is taken care of, too. All that's left then is a slight musky body fragrance that comes from the scent glands in a ferret's skin. And regular rub-a-dub-dubs in the tub will help control this leftover odor.

Be aware, however, that even when neutering has tamed the body odor problem, ferrets can still give you a smelly surprise by "poofing" stink bombs now and again. Ferrets have anal scent glands on either side of the rectum. These sacs are part of a ferret's defense mecha-nism—a strong, musky scent is released from them when a ferret becomes frightened or upset. Some ferrets also poof in their sleep or during playtime when they're really excited. Luckily, the offending smell dissipates quickly; it doesn't linger long like a skunk's stinky spray.

The only way to guarantee that your ferret will never let loose with a stink bomb is to have her descented. This means having the anal glands surgically removed. There are two schools of thought about this procedure. Some ferret enthusiasts are strongly opposed to descenting—they think it's unnecessary because most house ferrets rarely release the contents of their anal sacs. Other enthusiasts feel that descenting makes a ferret a more house friendly pet.

The majority of kits sold in North American pet shops come already descented, so most ferret owners don't have to make a choice. However, if you buy a ferret that hasn't been descented, read what you can about the descenting issue, talk to other owners, talk to your vet, then make your own decision.

Chapter Two

So You Want to Buy a Ferret . . .

Finding Your Ferret

You've done your homework and decided that a ferret's the right pet for you. Now where do you find the special furball that's to become part of your family? There are several options here—pet stores, breeders, or shelters—so once again, you have some research to do!

Most people buy their ferrets from pet stores. In years past, only specialty shops dealing in exotic animals carried ferrets. Today, however, they're widely available. If you can't find any ferrets at your local store, call around. You're bound to find one within driving distance.

Pet shops usually get their ferrets as babies (kits) from large commercial breeders. These kits are often bred for gentleness, so they make good family pets. In addition, they're usually neutered and descented and have had their first distemper shot. For a lot of people, this is the most convenient way to go—no decisions to make, no surgeries to arrange, no unexpected expenses. In the pet shop, you pick out your pet and pick up everything that you need to go with it.

Steer clear of stores where the assistants are not ferret knowledgeable. It's much better to make your pet purchase at a shop where the workers know about ferrets, can give you advice, and answer your questions. Chances are that the pet shop owner who keeps ferrets in a large cage with a litter box and soft bedding knows more about ferrets than someone who houses them in a tiny aquarium with no litter box and with cedar shavings for bedding.

In smaller pet shops, there might be only one or two ferrets for sale—not much of a choice for personality, gender, or color. Search out a shop that offers a choice. If you buy from a pet shop, be certain that the ferret has been frequently handled and well socialized by the staff. A kit that has spent its whole existence plopped in a cage may be people shy or darn right afraid of people. Also, make sure the ferret has had a litter box available from day one—this makes future litter box training a whole lot easier. Visit several pet shops and compare the quality of the ferrets, not just the price. A low price won't be a bargain if you end up with a kit that has behavior or health problems. Ask specifically about any health guarantees, and ask for written proof of any vaccinations that have already been given to the ferret.

Some people prefer to purchase their ferrets directly from a breeder. Breeders usually have kits for sale in season, from spring to fall. Sometimes, too, they have adults available whose reproductive years are over. Ferret breeders tend to specialize . . . some breed for size, some for temperament, some for championship bloodlines, others for colors or fur type. Some have bloodlines from different countries like the United Kingdom, Sweden, and Australia.

If you've set your heart on something specific or unusual ferret-wise, then your best bet might be to contact a reputable breeder. Unfortunately, this is easier said than done—you won't find a ferret breeder around every corner. So, how can you locate one? Try checking the advertisements in ferret magazines, contacting the ferret organizations, or surfing the Internet. Some breeders will ship ferrets to your home, others won't. However, if you're anxious to do your own pet picking and choosing, probably your biggest problem will be finding a breeder within reasonable driving distance. You might have to plan your summer vacation around ferretry visits. Just be sure to call and make appointments ahead of time.

Going the private breeder route can be a great way to get a ferret. Reputable breeders tend to handle and socialize their kits daily from a young age (as do some of the bigger commercial breeders). Some even hire people to do nothing but play with the youngsters, so you're liable to get a well-mannered, well-adjusted kit that's already hooked on humans. In most instances, you'll be able to take a look at the parents of any kit you want to purchase. Or, if the parents aren't around, the breeder should at least be able to fill you in on the details of their personalities, size, and health history—just ask. In fact, bring along a list of questions. A knowledgeable breeder won't mind being grilled (nicely) for information—as long as you're prepared to be grilled in return. Reputable breeders are picky—they won't let their charges go home with just anybody. They want buyers who will give their ferrets a good home.

Kits purchased from private breeders don't always come neutered and descented. Sometimes you have to sign a contract with the breeder agreeing to have the neutering done; sometimes the decision is left up to you. Should your fuzzy be fixed? Unless he or she is used for breeding, the answer is a definite YES! Why? For female ferrets, spaying can be a matter of life and death (see Chapter 15). And, besides, ferret shelters are already bursting at the seams with unwanted fuzzies. Don't add to the problem.

Although there's not much debate about whether a fuzzy should be fixed, there is a controversy about when to have the surgery done. Some ferret experts recommend that you wait until your ferret is six months old before you have it fixed. They think that early neutering and spaying—around six weeks of age—can lead to health problems later in a ferret's life. Other experts think that doing the procedure early ensures it gets done . . . and gets done before a female can come into heat. They claim there's no medical evidence to prove early neuters run a higher risk of medical problems. What's best for your furball? Read what you can about the issue, discuss it with your breeder and veterinarian, then make your decision.

Adopting a Rescue Ferret

Pet stores and breeders are the obvious places to make a ferret purchase. But for all the Good Samaritans out there, here's another A-1 option. Why not check out ferret shelters? Here you'll find deserving orphans looking for good homes. There are literally thousands of ferrets in shelters that would love to settle in with a new family. Young and old, male and female, healthy and sick—in shelters you'll find all

Check me out at the shelter. I'm looking for a good home.

types of ferrets. But they all have one thing in common . . . they're all looking for love. Don't assume that only "problem" ferrets find their way to shelters. Many wonderful ferrets end up in rescues through no fault of their own. How can they help it if their owners moved, lost a job, or just plain got tired of ferret duty?

Are there any advantages to getting a ferret from a shelter? You betcha! For starters, the workers are ferret knowledgeable. They can brief you on all the ins and outs, all the pros and cons, of ferret ownership *before* you commit yourself to a ferret purchase. Then, if you do decide to take the plunge, you'll have dozens of ferrets to choose from. When you've looked them over and drawn up your short list, you can spend time playing with them. Are you looking for a boisterous Bandit? Or, a sedate Serena? The workers can help here. They know the personalities of the individual ferrets, their litter box habits, their likes and dislikes, and how well they get on with other ferrets or other pets.

At shelters, you'll find more adult ferrets than kits, but buying an adult can have advantages. You won't have to get through the terrible twos, for one thing. Also, if you're looking to buy two ferrets, a shelter is a great place to pick out pets because you can be sure of finding two that have been around one another and won't fight.

Another advantage to buying a rescue ferret is cost. Usually the purchase price is cheaper than at pet shops or breeders, and for the icing on the cake, vaccinations are usually up to date. This doesn't mean, however, that shelter workers will hand over their precious charges to people who are interested only in buying a pet at a bargain price. When you go shelter shopping, there's not just the question of whether you'll find a suitable ferret. There's also the question of whether you're a suitable owner. Expect an interview. Not everybody who shows up at a ferret shelter will leave with a pet in hand.

Another major bonus of buying from a shelter is that you can phone up if you're having any problems—workers are a good source of accurate ferret information. And finally, there's the feel-good factor . . . you've given a home to a ferret that would otherwise have been lost in the shuffle of life.

Male or Female?

When you're picking a ferret, you might think that your first important decision is whether to buy a male or a female. But in point of fact, you can pick out whichever ferret takes your fancy without worrying about its sex, because either a male or a female will make a great pet.

Male ferrets are known as hobs and neutered males are called gibs, although the word hob is commonly used for both. Males are usually bigger than females. Their average weight ranges anywhere from 2.5 to 4 pounds (approximately 1.1 kg to

Are you looking for a male . . .

1.8 kg), though the runt of a litter can be smaller. Then there are the big-boy ferrets. Some breeders specialize in 6-pound (2.7 kg) whoppers—European stock is often imported to bring size into the bloodlines. Swedish ferrets are particularly popular because large size is genetically determined.

Males that aren't neutered have greasy fur and a distinctive musky smell. They're also more aggressive. However, most pet ferrets are neutered. The neutering takes care of the grease, the stink, and the aggression.

Female ferrets are called jills; if they're spayed they're called sprites. But most people use the word jill for all females. Females are generally smaller than males—in the 0.75 to 2.5 pound (0.3 to 1.1 kg) range.

. . . or a female?

Unspayed jills have a pronounced smell and greasy fur when in season—spaying will take care of this. And anyway, jills should be spayed if not kept for breeding, because unfixed female ferrets can develop life-threatening health problems (see Chapter 15). Most female ferrets in the United States are sold already spayed. If you buy one that isn't fixed, realize that the cost of spaying a female is usually higher than the cost of neutering a male.

With bright eyes and a shiny coat, Jake is a picture of health.

Some people are hooked on hobs; others are fans of females. All you need to know is that there really isn't any difference between male and female ferrets as pets . . . it's just a matter of personal choice. The bottom line is it's the personality of the individual ferret that's important, not the sex.

One or More?

Is yours to be a one-ferret family? Or would you prefer two ferrets? Or three? Are you planning to buy one now and add another to the household later? There's more to these questions than meets the eye. In fact, there's so much more that a whole chapter is devoted to the issue. Better skip ahead to Chapter 10 on page 89 before you make these all-important decisions.

Signs of a Healthy Ferret

Now you know where to find a ferret, but what should you be looking for when choosing your particular pal? First off, you need to pick a healthy pet. And how will you recognize a healthy one? Although some health problems aren't obvious, here are some guidelines to help you in your search. Look for a ferret that has clear, bright eyes and a full, shiny coat. Any bald spots on the body or any lumps, bumps, or wartlike growths could indicate a health problem. There should be no discharges from the eyes, nose, or anus. Check the inside of the ears, too. Is there any wax buildup? A little is normal, but gobs of goo could mean a problem with ear mites.

Next, look at the ferret's teeth. Are they discolored or crooked? Crooked teeth can be difficult to clean; protruding teeth or overbites can cause lip sores that are hard to heal. Are any teeth broken? Realize that broken teeth may need expensive dental work. Count the fingers and toes. If there are more than five per paw, this is unusual but not a health concern—you'll just have extra toenails to clip.

What about that ferret shivering in the corner of the cage? Is something wrong with him? Is he cold or frightened? Probably not. A shivering, trembling ferret is perfectly normal—it's neither frightened nor frozen. Ferrets shiver when they're excited and when they first wake up. All ferrets do it; it's usually nothing to worry about.

What about that crazy little cutie who's leaping up and bouncing around, scuttling backward, jumping straight up in the air, rolling over, dooking, and generally acting like a mad thing? Has he whacked his head? Does he have rabies? Naaa, he's just happy, full of life, and doing the ferret war dance. Most ferrets do this when all's well with their world—count this as a plus when you're picking your pet. You *want* a ferret that's active and alert . . . this is a sign of good health.

Ferrets do sleep a lot, and they sleep deeply. You might even have trouble waking one up. This is known as the *dead ferret syndrome*—when a perfectly healthy ferret looks and acts dead to the world. It's nothing to be concerned about as long as the ferret is lively and playful when awake.

Now look past the ferret and check the litter box. A ferret's stools are frequently a good indicator of his general health. Normal stools should be well formed, tubular, and medium brown in color. Are there any loose stools in the litter box? Are there any green or blood-tinged ones? Do the stools look as if they're full of bird seeds? If so, play it safe—pick your pet elsewhere.

If, however, you see the ferret of your dreams dragging his bottom after using the litter box, don't worry. This is normal. It doesn't mean worms! It's just a ferret's way of wiping his bottom because ferret toilet paper isn't easy to come by.

Reputable pet shops and breeders won't knowingly sell sick ferrets. Most kits come with a limited health guarantee. This varies from shop to shop and breeder to breeder, so be sure to ask for details. The story at shelters is a little different. Although they certainly have plenty of healthy ferrets for adoption, they will sometimes let ailing ferrets be adopted by people who have the commitment, knowledge, and experience to look after them.

A Winning Personality

Another important consideration when choosing a ferret is to look for one that has the type of personality that chimes with yours. Are you looking for a ferret that's a bundle of energy? Check out little Scooter who's cavorting about the cage non-stop, leaping through tunnels, and hurdling over his littermates—he makes you tired just looking at him. Or, are you leaning more toward a mild-mannered little sweetheart? Check out easygoing Edgar, the one that's asleep in a heap and cuddles close when you hold him. But make sure you check out Edgar a few hours later when he's totally awake—he could be a wolf in sheep's clothing, a proper little spit-fire when he's not snoozing. To avoid an owner/ferret mismatch, check out your chosen companion several times a day, at different times of the day, so you can assess his true personality.

Look for a good temperament. Active is OK, but think twice about a truly hyperactive ferret that could need a lot of behavior training. Kits sometimes nip lightly and/or mouth fingers, but a kit that clamps down with gusto and won't let go isn't the best bet for the first-time ferret owner. The same goes for the bully boy who insists on dragging his brothers and sisters around the cage by the neck. The two of you might lock horns when it comes to deciding who's boss.

Time spent finding the ferret that's right for you is time well spent because you'll be spending a lot of years together. Give yourself the best-possible start. If the first ferrets you see don't seem to be what you're looking for, don't feel oblig-ated to pick from that particular bunch. Look elsewhere, or go back next month when another litter is available for inspection. It's better to wait for Mr. Right than to be stuck for years with Mr. Wrong.

Color Choices

The good health and personality of a ferret are certainly the most important issues when choosing one. But those personalities can come in a wide range of colors and patterns. Until recently, the available ferrets were mainly sable colored or albino. But over the last few years, ferret breeders have been aiming for more unusual colors and/or pat-terns. The descriptions given here are general. They are not meant to be specifications for show stan-dards, as different show venues may have slightly different requirements for each category of color or pattern. For specific information on show standards, check with the club host-ing the show.

So what's out there color-wise? The most common ferret color is sable. The undercoat (the dense, soft fur close to the body) is white-to-cream or yellow, while the guard hairs (the long hairs that cover the

A sable is a warm, rich brown with a raccoonlike mask.

undercoat) are a warm, rich, dark brown. In a sable ferret, the typical raccoonlike face mask is very prominent. The eyes are brown to black, and the nose can be pink, light brown, black, or mottled. When most people think *ferret,* it's a sable they have in mind.

A black sable is just what it sounds like—black. The guard hairs are a deep, dark blue-black with little or none of the white-to-cream undercoat showing through. The nose and the mask should be as black as possible, and the eyes are dark brown to black.

On the lighter side, there's a chocolate sable. Think of the color of chocolate milk and you'll get the picture. Chocolates have a white-to-cream to wheat-colored undercoat, black or ruby eyes, and a pink-to-beige-to-light-brown nose.

More unusual yet are cinnamon ferrets. These are a definite reddish brown color, just like a stick of cinnamon. Some are even Irish Setter red . . . real eye-catchers. For the undercoat, a golden color is preferred, but buff to creamy white is just fine. The mask is usually pale, and some cinnamons have no mask at all. Eyes of deep ruby red or black, and a nose that's brick colored, beige, or pink complete the picture.

Other specialty colors are champagne and butterscotch. Champagne ferrets have tan-beige-colored topcoats, white or cream undercoats, ruby red eyes, and pink or beige noses. Butterscotch ferrets are—you've guessed it—butterscotch! At least their guard hairs are, while the underfur is creamy colored to yellow.

Another common ferret is the albino. Due to a recessive gene, these ferrets have a true absence of pigment. They have a white undercoat, white guard hairs, a pink nose, and pink eyes. True albinos have no colored hairs at all in their fur, although the fur itself can change from white to a creamy yellow as the ferret ages. Albinos can also be pure white in the winter and yellowish in the summer. Unaltered males can be almost totally yellow in appearance due to the oils secreted by their skin glands.

Albinos are not to be confused with black-eyed or blue-eyed whites. These guys are all white or creamy like an albino, but their eyes are a deep burgundy or blue. Dark-eyed whites can also have a few black guard hairs where true albinos do not.

Sterling silver and pewter ferrets are both gray in color, sterling being the lighter of the two. Pewter, also known as heavy silver, is a deep gun-metal gray. On silvers, masks are usually absent or look like smudges around the eyes—ferrets are party animals, you know. The eyes themselves are dark, and noses can be pink, speckled, or black.

Is your head spinning yet? Hang in there—there are even more color confusions and complications to consider. Did you know that a ferret's color can vary with the season of the year? That kit you chose so carefully in the summer could look quite a bit different when he's wearing his heavier winter coat. A ferret's color can also change with age. Would you believe that your sterling-silver showstopper could be completely white later in life?

Now that you're thoroughly confused about colors, it's time to add patterns to the mix. Not only do ferrets come in a variety of colors, each color can be found in a variety of patterns. For example, mitted ferrets can be found in any of the above-mentioned colors except white. Mitted ferrets have white feet—they look as if they're wearing socks. A silver mitt would be a silver-colored ferret with four white feet. And the socks on those feet could be long ones or short ones. Many mitts also have white bibs and knee patches, as well as a white tip to their tails.

A ferret with a blaze or badger pattern will have a long white stripe starting at the forehead and going down between the ears to the shoulders. A white bib and four white mitts complete the picture, with white knee patches considered a plus. No full masks allowed—only eye rings.

A panda ferret's body can be any of the standard colors, but its head must be almost completely white from nose to shoulder. It also has to have a full white bib. A fully dressed

This butterscotch ferret is a standout!

panda must have those four white socks, and many have matching white tail tips. Unfortunately, along with their striking appearance, pandas and blazes do have a genetic propensity to deafness.

Are you partial to the markings on Siamese cats? Then how about a similarly patterned ferret? Siamese ferrets can be any standard color other than black or white, but the legs and tail must be several shades darker than the body. The mask, which is thin and V shaped, is the same darker color as the tail tip and legs.

If you like the look of a Dalmatian dog, then a Dalmatian ferret could be right up your alley. Not very common, but quite distinctive, these ferrets are white with dark spots or blotches. Are stripes more your style? Then a striped ferret could be for you. These are dark-eyed whites with a definite dark stripe extending right down their backs and sometimes onto their tails.

If spots and stripes don't tickle your fancy, how about the more subtle salt-and-pepper pattern of roan ferrets? These ferrets can be any color, but 50 percent of their guard hairs will be white. They are quite handsome, especially in darker colors like black, chocolate, or pewter.

Lots of ferrets don't conform to strict show standards. It's OK for you to call your Patch a silver mitt even though he has three white feet instead of four. With ferrets becoming more and more popular as pets, breeders all over the world are developing new colors, patterns, and fur types. Long-haired angoras are already available. Who knows when a blue or lilac ferret will show up? But please keep in mind that fur color is only skin deep. Color, pattern, and fur type are on the outside . . . it's what's on the inside that counts. Gentleness and a sweet disposition are infinitely more important than your ferret's coat color.

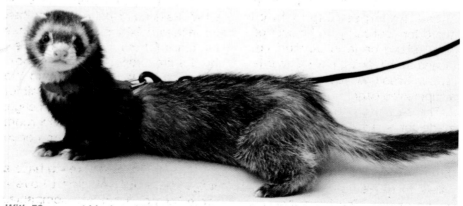

With 50 percent black and 50 percent white guard hairs, Money has the salt-and-pepper appearance of a roan.

Chapter Three

Housing

Choosing a Cage

Home sweet home. What does this mean to your ferret? It means she needs a great cage to call her own. Even if your ferret runs free in the house all day long, even if she has a one-room ferret playroom designated just for her, it's in her best interest safety-wise to cage her when you're asleep or out of the house. Why? Because accidents can happen no matter how well you've ferret proofed the house (see Chapter 6).

So what kind of cage are you looking for? Aim for a castle, not a hovel. It's really important to purchase the largest cage you can afford for your fuzzy. If the cost of a good-sized cage is beyond your means at this point, put off your ferret purchase until you can spring for a supersized cage.

The best cage for a ferret is one made for a ferret. These specialty cages have the wires or bars spaced just right for furballs and have been ferret tested and approved. Fortunately, there are now lots of choices on the market. You'll find that most ferret cages are vinyl-, powder-, chrome-, or epoxy-coated wire. Stay away from galvanized cages because your ferret may be a cage climber or a chewer. If she chews galvanized wire, she could get zinc poisoning; if she climbs the wires and then licks her paws, again she could get zinc poisoning. No ferret cages on your local pet store shelves? You could have the store manager order one for you. Or you could check the ferret magazines at pet stores for cage advertisements. Are you on the Net? Try surfing for ferret stores or cage companies that will deliver a suitable cage right to your front door.

What are you looking for size-wise? Pass up anything smaller than 36 inches × 24 inches × 24 inches (90 cm × 60 cm × 60 cm). After all, by the time you put in a litter box, bowls, tunnels, bedding, and the toys, how much space will be left for the ferret? When it comes to a cage, bigger is better. If you have room and money for a huge ferret condo or penthouse, go for it!

If you'd like your ferret to have a large cage but you don't have a large budget, there are companies that sell building block cages. Start

Ferrets do best in a large cage.

friendly. You may have to do some renovating. For example, if the cage you buy comes with a wire floor, this is not good for ferret feet. Wire floors are hard on tender tootsies. Sometimes the wire floor is removable—if so, take it out. It doesn't come out? Then cover it up with a measured-to-fit carpet mat. Make sure the mat is removable for easy washing, and make sure it doesn't have a rubber backing—ferrets love to snack on rubber, but it can be hazardous to their health.

Some cages have metal or plastic floors. These will do in a pinch so long as you pile in cozy bedding. But ferrets tend to slip and slide on plastic and metal. For sure footing and cozy comfort, measure the inside of the cage and buy a carpet mat to fit. You can buy them very cheaply at the dollar store, discount store, or flea market. Don't glue the mat down because it will need to be washed on a regular basis. Of course, washing will make the carpet's jute backing go limp, but what the heck—it's comfort, not looks that your critter cares about. After you've hand washed the mat, give it a quick spin dry in the washer, then hang it up to air dry. In fact, it's a good idea to buy two mats so you have one for the cage while the other's drip drying.

out with section #1 this month, order section #2 next month, and buy section #3 for your ferret's birthday. Again, check the Internet for companies that sell expandable ferret cages, or look through ads in ferret magazines.

If you're going to order a cage sight unseen, first make a model out of cardboard to the exact dimensions. Is it the size you envisioned? Or is it a lot smaller than you thought it would be? Is it *really* big enough for an energetic ferret? Will it fit next to the bookcase in the family room as you had anticipated?

Don't assume that all cages made for ferrets are completely ferret

You could also buy a chenille throw rug or a rag rug for the cage floor. Either of these are good alternatives to carpets. They'll bunch up a bit on the floor, but, hey, they're easy to wash and cheap to replace.

Steer clear of these, though, if your ferret's a material muncher.

A multilevel cage is best for ferrets because there's more roam room. But here again, you might have to doctor up the ladders and platforms that come with the cage. Plastic or metal platforms can be slippery for rambunctious ferrets; wire platforms, like wire floors, aren't critter comfortable or ferret foot friendly. The best plan is to cover them up. Don't, however, cover them with loose bedding that could slide right off, ferret and all. Fitted covers are the way to go.

Some manufacturers make special shelf covers. But if homemade fits your budget better than ready-made, here are some platform cover-up ideas. Hockey socks slip right over most shelves. They can easily be cut to fit and hemmed, and it's a breeze to get them off for washing. You can also make slip-covers for the platforms. Buy thick, fleecy material and sew it into a tube shape to pull over the platform. Better yet, instead of stitching the tube seam closed, use Velcro to hold the two edges together. This way you won't have to remove the platform to get the cover off . . . you can just rip the Velcro apart (see photo).

You could also carpet the shelves with a short-napped, commercial-grade carpet. Just make sure it doesn't have a rubber backing that your ferret could chew off and swallow. Stick the carpet down with non-toxic glue. This option is cheap and easy, but there is a drawback. After

Your pet will enjoy stretching her legs in a multilevel cage.

A ferret cage should be no smaller than 36 inches (90 cm) × 24 inches (60 cm) × 24 inches (60 cm).

When a shelf cover's fastened with Velcro, it's a cinch to remove for cleaning.

it's glued down, you can't remove the carpet to clean it . . . you have to remove the shelf in order to clean the carpet that's stuck to it. Of course, your ferret won't have use of the shelf while the carpet's drying—she'll be confined to the basement level while the upper stories are hanging out to dry.

When you put together that tall, multilevel cage, take a look at how the shelves are arranged. Is there free fall space from the top platforms to the cage floor? Is the drop so great that your ferret could get injured if she jumped or fell? If so,

Ferrets won't slip on wire ladders that are covered with hockey socks.

add a hammock or two in the danger zones to catch free-falling ferrets.

Most ferrets find wire ladders a bit awkward to navigate. But cover those ladders with hockey socks or carpet, and your fuzzy will be racing up and down in no time. Now take a look at the angle of the ladders. Is it too steep? If so, make sure to reposition the platforms so that the ladder slope is gentler.

Is your ferret not too sure about climbing ramps or ladders? You might have to teach her how. Keep coaxing her up with a treat a little at a time until she can run up the ramp on her own. After all, if you've scrimped and scraped to buy a four-story ferret condo, you don't want the tenant skulking on the ground floor and missing out on the penthouse view.

One last note on ferret cages . . . double check those latches. Ferrets are real escape artists. Should yours show any interest in undoing the door, don't wait until she's figured out how; clip on a spring hook and stymie her efforts.

Are there any other types of cage suitable for a ferret? Most small-animal cages are definitely too small. Plastic dog travel carriers, even the large ones, are also too cramped and claustrophobic. What about that wire dog crate you've got stored in the garage? Forget it—the wires will probably be too far apart to keep in wily weasels.

Aquariums are not a good idea for ferrets either. There's not enough room or ventilation in the small ones.

And the large ones are expensive, heavy, unwieldy to move, and difficult to customize. Have you ever tried attaching a platform to an aquarium wall?

Bedding

Ferrets like soft, cozy bedding to sleep in. Forget wood shavings in the cage—save those for hamsters and gerbils. Soft carpet on the floor and blankies to snooze on are the way to go for the modern ferret.

Sleeping bags are a big hit with ferrets, too. You can find luxurious ready-mades for your furball to wallow in, or it's easy and cheap to make your own. Buy a remnant approximately 15 inches × 30 inches (40 cm × 75 cm). Anything thick, soft, plush, and washable will do nicely. Fold it in half, and stitch up the side seams. If sewing isn't your forte, cut off the leg(s) of an old pair of sweatpants. A discarded hockey sock or a fuzzy baby blanket will also bring a smile to your ferret's face.

Don't use terry cloth towels for bedding because toenails can get caught in the loops. And when using old clothing, remove any buttons, bows, elastic, or fasteners before your ferret does. As for hole-ridden castoffs, toss them into the rag bag rather than into the ferret cage because a burrowing Bandit could get her head stuck in a hole.

Is your fuzzy showing any interest in eating her cloth bedding? Then you'll have to remove the fabric right away before she does a chew and swallow. Swallowing material can result in intestinal obstruction and cause a medical emergency. Material munching is more commonly seen in kits. Don't ever keep a kit in cloth bedding if she shows any sign of doing a taste test. Instead, issue her with alternative bedding such as a cardboard box. When she's a few months older, you can introduce her to cloth again, but only under close supervision—many kits grow out of their fabric fetish. For the cloth addicts that don't, you'll need to provide a cardboard box, a plastic tube, or a ferret ball for naps.

Bottles and Bowls

Crunch, crunch, slurp, slurp—is your ferret a regular little munching machine? Ferrets eat roughly every four hours, so food and water have to be available to them around the

No wood shavings, please—ferrets need soft, warm bedding.

23

Ferrets like to move their bowls around—buy something heavy that will stay put.

clock. But you can't dish up their dinner in just any old dish because most ferrets think it's great fun to pull, push, flip, tip, drag, and dump any free-standing dish they can get their paws onto. You can foil this ferret fun—and save yourself a lot of cleanup—by careful selection of dishes and bowls.

For water, sipper bottles are a good choice. A heavy plastic one that holds about 16 ounces (475 mL) of water will be fine for one or two ferrets. For more ferrets, or for a multilevel cage, you might need to buy more than one bottle. Most ferrets take to a sipper bottle like ducks to water, but some kits don't clue in right away. When you bring home a baby ferret, watch carefully to see that she knows what that tube poking through the cage wires is for and that she's actually drinking from it. You might have to show her how it's done. No, you don't have to crawl under the tube yourself and demonstrate—just place her mouth under

the tube and flip the ball bearing with your fingertip. She'll catch on in no time.

Before hanging the sipper bottle onto the side of the cage, fill it right up to the top with water. This creates a vacuum and prevents the bottle from leaking—you hope. If your hopes aren't realized and it drip, drip, drips, return the sipper to the store and try a different model. Don't be stung again. Why not top up and test the bottle at the pet store before bringing it home? When installing the bottle, attach it to the cage wires so that it's at a comfortable angle for your pet—too low and she can't get at the water, too high and she'll get a crick in her neck.

The other way to provide water is in a bowl. Some ferrets will drink more readily from a bowl than from a sipper bottle. But there can be a problem with bowls—ferrets like to rearrange their cage contents according to their whim of the day. Bowls are a prime target, and water tends to slosh when it's moved. So if a free-standing bowl is what you're planning on, make it a heavy-duty, nonslip, nontip, nonflip, ferret-proof bowl. Heavy ceramic or mock marble are your best bets, but even these aren't guaranteed to stay put if you've got a big mover and shaker. Is there any way to keep the bowl in place? Fortunately, yes. Use cage clips. Attach these to the bowl and to the cage wires. Then even the most determined ferret won't be able to move the bowl. But keep a spare package of clips on hand in case the ones on the bowl eventually lose their stick.

Are there any other water bowl options? There certainly are. Probably the best ferret bowls available are those that lock onto the sides of the cage. When locked on properly, they're immovable and spill proof. Croc-Lok or Smart Croc are examples of what you're looking for. Ask for them in either the small animal or bird department at pet supply stores.

In fact, buy two of these locked bowls and use one for water, the other for food. Ferrets aren't picky about which bowl they overturn—they're just as happy scattering food as they are sloshing water. So, it's equally important to batten down the food bowls as it is to anchor the water bowls. Bowls aren't the only food containers you can attach to the side of the cage. J feeders or bin feeders are another food delivery system that many ferret owners opt for.

Ferrets that roam far from their cage should have food and water

Bowls that lock onto the cage are a best buy.

available elsewhere in the house. For these dash and dine stations, food and water containers that lock or clamp to the cage bars won't do. After all, you can't attach them to the kitchen floor. The best option here is to spring for the heaviest ceramic or mock marble bowls you can find. Stay away from the stainless steel bowls that have nonskid rubber around the bottom—ferrets eat rubber.

Here's a hygiene hint—keep all food and water containers clean, clean, clean. Bacteria and slime love to hide in dirty bowls, and sippers can stop working if clogged with gunk.

Litter Boxes

It's important to start out the right way with litter training, and starting the right way means having a litter box in the cage at all times. Don't ever put your ferret into her cage unless there's a litter box ready and waiting. Otherwise, your ferret will develop bad habits that are difficult to change. For all the ins and outs and ups and downs of litter training, see Chapter 7. Read it twice!

Cage Accessories

There are two types of cage accessories—those that cater to your ferret's comfort and those that add fun to your ferret's cage time. Does your pet spend a lot of time in her cage? Then you shouldn't look at accessories as optional extras but as necessities. Even a fuzzy that doesn't hang around in her cage much will appreciate having some home comforts and amusements. You can really go to town when you're jazzin' up the cage. However, if the piggy bank's empty after you've splurged on the cage itself, don't worry. Accessories needn't be expensive.

Most ferrets love lounging in hammocks. A cage seems empty

A cage is not complete without a hammock or two.

without at least one. There are some snazzy, ready-made, fur-lined hammocks on the market—your furball will be in seventh heaven in one of these fashionable, furry hangouts. Or, you could sew one up yourself for a few dollars. Your ferret won't notice if the seams are straight or not. Are your fingers all thumbs when it comes to sewing? You can quickly rig up a pseudohammock by tying knots in the four corners of a dish towel, then tying heavy-duty shoestrings to the base of the knots, and attaching the other ends of the shoestrings to the cage wires. Just be absolutely certain that the knots are tied securely—or down will come fuzzy, hammock and all.

Other ferret favorites are soft cloth tunnels and sleep sacks, either parked at ground level or hanging from the rafters. Again, you can go the store-bought route if you want a designer special—can you picture your ferret in a hot air balloon? Or, you can stick to homemade. Cut a leg off a pair of blue jeans or sweatpants for an instant tunnel.

In the home entertainment line, what will tickle Fuzzy's fancy? Try large plastic ferret balls, small ferret treat balls, playhouses, Ping-Pong balls, spongy jumpers, and giant roll-a-nests. One of the best homemade toys for the cage is a ferret chew bone tied to a heavy shoelace and dangled near floor level. Watch the ferrets swat it, bat it, grab it, and roll around with it. Another good idea is to provide your pet with a piece of black plastic corrugated draining tube cut to a length that will fit her cage (check your local building supply store or lumberyard).

These are just a few ferret fun ideas. What can you come up with?

Selecting a Site

Ferrets are sociable animals; they like to feel that they're part of the family. So don't stick the cage into the basement. Choose a location where the curious critters will be right at the center of family life— somewhere where they'll be safe and comfortable, somewhere where their quality of life will be good. And this doesn't mean right next to the subwoofer or junior's drum set!

When selecting a site, keep in mind the fact that many ferrets like to scale to new heights by climbing the outside of their cages. From the cage summit, a wily weasel can then take a flying leap to the wall unit, the computer desk, to the top of the television, or to anything else that's conveniently close. If you have a cage climber, make sure she can't clamber up the cage to reach places that are off limits.

Choose a site where your ferret has no chance of being overheated. Ferrets DO NOT tolerate heat (see Chapter 15). The cage needs to be kept well away from direct sunlight, wood stoves, fireplaces, radiators, and heating vents. It shouldn't be in a hot, steamy bathroom, either. Avoid drafty corners, too. Keep the

Up, up, and away!

cage away from air-conditioning vents or units and away from open windows.

For your own convenience, locate Fuzzy's house where it's easy for you to clean house—hers and yours. You don't want the cage surrounded by so much furniture that you can't get at it. And when you've found a good location, stick with it. Ferrets aren't nomads . . . they like to know where their beds are at night.

Chapter Four

Ferret Nutrition

The Importance of Having the Right Food

Ferrets have very precise nutritional needs. Research shows that feeding your fuzzy leftover table food or dog food just won't do. Why not? Neither contains the nutrients that ferrets need. Some high-quality cat or kitten foods might be acceptable, but you'd better read the list of ingredients very carefully and check with your veterinarian. Anyway, with all of the good-quality ferret foods available, why use anything else?

Ferret Foods

In years past, ferret food was hard to find. But nowadays, it's stocked in most pet stores, or you can special order it, mail order it, or Internet order it.

Ferrets need a diet that is very high in animal protein. The listing for protein on the back of the package should be between 32 percent and 38 percent, while the fat content should be between 18 percent and 22 percent. The main ingredients, listed first on the package, should come from animal sources like poultry, meat meal, and fish rather than from plant protein such as corn. This is because ferrets are obligate carnivores and their food *must* contain a high percentage of quality animal protein if they're to be healthy. Eating too much plant protein won't give ferrets the nutrients they need and may make them susceptible to urinary tract stones. Many authorities also recommend that taurine be included in the list of ingredients because it is believed that taurine helps reduce the chance of heart disease in ferrets.

The best way to ensure that your ferret is getting a proper diet is to buy good-quality, name brand, ferret-specific food such as Eight In One, Fluker's, Kaytee, Marshall Farms, Mazuri, Path Valley, Sun Seed, or Totally Ferret.

Don't economize on your ferret's food. Buying low quality is a false economy because your fuzzy would have to eat twice as much to get the nutrients he needs. But most likely, he wouldn't be able to eat twice as much, so his health would suffer. And anyway, your ferret(s) won't eat you out of house and home, so even buying the best ferret food you can lay your hands on won't make much of a dent in your budget.

Lots of ferrets are very picky eaters. They get used to one food and refuse to eat another. This is bad news if your pet's favorite food vanishes from the store shelves. How do you avoid a hunger strike? Right from the day you bring that critter home, start him off on a mix of three different ferret foods. This way, if Brand #1 is discontinued, you won't have an obstinate, hungry ferret on your hands . . . he'll still eat the mix of Brand #2 and Brand #3. If you find that your food snob gobbles up two of the brands and always turns up his nose at the third, try another brand in its place. Nowadays, it's not hard to lay your hands on several different brands of high-quality ferret food—if not at pet stores then at least by snail mail or e-mail.

What about canned ferret foods? Are they OK? They are, but you might not think so from reading the labels. For example, on a can of ferret food, you'll usually see the protein listed at 9 percent to 10 percent. How can this be OK for your ferret when you know that he needs between 32 percent and 38 percent protein? In actual fact, the protein content of both canned food and dry food is about the same—the percentage difference on the labels is due to the moisture content of the canned food.

Even though canned food is good for furballs, they shouldn't eat only canned food and nothing else. Ferrets need to crunch and munch on dry food to keep their teeth and gums healthy. So, the best thing to do with soft ferret food is to serve it in small portions to supplement the regular diet of dry food. Don't stockpile a large supply of canned food until you find out if your ferret likes it. Some ferrets are crazy about it, others can't stand

With the right food, your ferret will be bouncing with energy.

Crunching dry food keeps your pet's teeth clean.

the stuff. Does your fuzzy find it to his fancy? Give him a bowl of it at lunchtime. Just make sure that what he doesn't finish goes into the fridge. You can't leave it sitting out like dry food.

Is your furball getting fat? Could it be all this good food? Before you put him on a diet, have him checked out at the vet—it's not just overeating that can make a ferret fat. He could be chubby due to lack of exercise, he might be overeating due to boredom if he's spending too much time in the cage, or he could look overweight due to a medical condition. If he's older and less active, his diet could be too high in protein and fat now. Before you do anything to help your fuzzy reduce, the vet will have to determine the cause of that portly paunch. The remedy might be as easy as increasing your pet's exercise time every day or switching

him to a ferret food specially developed for older ferrets. Food that has 30 percent to 33 percent protein and 15 percent to 18 percent fat may be more suitable for an elderly ferret. Whatever you do, don't restrict your ferret's food intake to one or two meals a day. Ferrets are not like cats or dogs—they *need* to eat every three to four hours.

If you're a vegetarian, please, please don't try to make your furball one, too. It just won't work—ferrets are carnivores and need meat products to stay healthy. Their digestive systems can't extract enough nutrients from plant materials to meet their nutritional needs. A ferret on a vegetarian diet will slowly starve.

Free Choice of Food and Water

Ferrets have a short digestive tract; what they take in at one end will reappear, in poop form, at the other end in just three or four hours. For this reason, your bottomless pit will need to eat five or six times a day. If he doesn't, he'll be hungry. Having dry food available free choice allows a ferret to eat whenever he's hungry and keeps his insides healthy.

Along with the food, your pet will need to have water available at all times. This is very important because ferrets won't eat food unless they can take a few sips of water after every couple of nibbles . . . nibble,

nibble, lap, lap. Therefore, the food and water dishes should be placed side by side, not across the cage from one another or on different levels.

With the dishes side-by-side, your ferret's liable to drip water into the food dish as he goes back and forth between food and water. The food pellets will absorb the water. Over time, the damp pellets can become moldy, especially if you keep topping up the dish with fresh food instead of cleaning it out regularly. So, check the food bowl frequently, and remove the soggy pieces.

Is your water high in sulfur, iron, or other minerals? Does it taste bad to you? Don't expect your ferret to swig it back eagerly, either. Better give him bottled water instead, or he may not drink as much as he needs. And if your house water goes through a water softener, make sure your ferret gets the same drinking water as you—softened water may have high levels of salt that aren't good for your pet.

And what sort of treats have ferret appeal? Not every ferret likes the same stuff, so you'll probably have to experiment a bit to find treats that your fuzzy will do flip-flops for. A good place to start is in the ferret section of the pet store. Look for liquid skin and coat supplements like Ferret Derm, Ferretone, Furo-Tone, Linatone for ferrets, Pet Derm, and Vet's Best Healthy Coat Supplement. These supplements contain vitamins and fatty acids that will keep your ferret's skin healthy and his fur gleaming. The label will tell you exactly how much your ferret can have every day. What the label won't tell you is that ferrets absolutely adore these products . . . put a few drops onto a plastic spoon and you can train a ferret to do just about anything. The same goes for vitamin supplements such as Ferretvite, Furo-vite, or Nutrical. Again, it's a rare ferret that won't turn cartwheels for these.

The different brands of fatty acid and vitamin supplements all have slightly different tastes . . . some are

Good Treats

As long as you're feeding that furball a high-quality ferret food, then he doesn't need anything else in his diet for good health. However, let's face it . . . sensible eating can be boring eating. Why not add a treat or two to brighten up your pet's day?

Ferrets eat every three to four hours. Food and water should be available to them around the clock.

Yum, yum . . . lemme at 'em!

supplement onto his lips so he can lick it off. Before long, he'll be begging for it. Then you're on to a good thing because if your fuzzy ever needs medicine, you can mix the medicine into the supplement and your ferret will lap it right up.

Two words of warning. First, don't dish out any supplements without reading the instructions carefully and calculating the exact dosage according to the package directions. Too much of a good thing can end up being a bad thing—you don't want to overdose your pet on vitamins. Second, keep all tubes of vitamin supplements well out of ferret reach. There have been reports of ferret thieves that have stolen and stashed a tube, then gobbled up the whole thing, tube and all. Unfortunately, feasts like this can be fatal because pieces of the plastic tube can cause intestinal obstruction.

fishier than others. A fastidious ferret might prefer one flavor over another. Realize, too, that for the occasional kit, supplements are an acquired taste. If your kit doesn't take to the bottle or the tube at first, rub a little

Fatty acid and vitamin supplements aren't the only ferret treats on pet store shelves. In recent years, a wide variety of just-for-your-ferret goodies has become available. Again, not all ferrets will like everything that's out there. Your galloping gourmet is not necessarily going to go crackers over the same treats your friend's ferrets gobble with gusto. Trial and error is the name of the game.

Store bought isn't the only way to go, either. Your refrigerator and kitchen pantry will have food to tickle ferret taste buds. Remember that ferrets need a lot of animal protein, so you can't go wrong with small pieces

Skin and coat supplements are not only delicious, they're good for your ferret, too.

Small bits of fruits and vegetables appeal to some ferrets.

of cooked chicken, liver, fish, or meat (no bones). Or how about chicken, veal, or turkey baby food? For a real lip-smacking desert, why not dish up a ferret sundae—one dollop of chicken baby food, dribbled with a little Ferretone "sauce," and topped off with a raisin "cherry"?

Bite-sized pieces of fruits and vegetables are OK in small quantities. Although they don't have the same nutritional value for ferrets as they do for people, they can certainly add a little spice to your pet's life. Some ferrets have been known to go gaga over green peppers—or cucumbers without the skin, cooked green peas, chopped broccoli, cooked green beans, chopped up snow peas, tomatoes, quartered grapes, apple pieces, kiwi, pear bits, cantaloupe, watermelon, blueberries, or mashed bananas. Dried fruits, such as bananas, pears, pineapple, apricots, and raisins (a big ferret favorite) can be cut into very small pieces and given sparingly. Too much of this sugar-rich food is bad for the teeth.

The odd Cheerio (no sugar coatings, please), low-salt cracker, cooked pasta, or tiny bit of toast are OK. Just don't overdo it; ferrets digest carbohydrates and fiber poorly.

Keep in mind that treats are just that—treats. They're certainly not substitutes for what your furball should be eating every day. Keep them to a minimum.

And Stay Away From . . .

There are lots of treats that are OK for ferrets. There are also lots of treats that ferrets love that aren't OK for them.

Don't give your pet any foods that are high in sugar. No cake, no cookies, no candy, no sugary cereals. Not only are these bad for the teeth, there are reported cases of ferrets getting diabetes when they've been overindulged and eaten too much sugar. Chocolate also makes the no-no list for its sugar content, but it's a no-no for another reason, too. There are stimulants in chocolate than people can handle but ferrets cannot.

It's an odd ferret that doesn't *luuvv* red licorice. You know, the cheap twisted-stick kind. Should you give some to Fuzzy? The strict ferret nutritionist will say, "Of course not." But the ferret lover in you will probably bend the rules once in a while. Don't feel guilty, but don't bend them too often. And, when you do cave in, cut the licorice up small and be stingy with the amounts.

Salty treats aren't good for you and they aren't good for your four-legged friend. So cut out the chips, nix the nachos, and pass up the pretzels. Pass up the popcorn, too; the popped puffy pieces can get stuck in greedy gullets.

A lot of ferrets like dairy products, but dairy products don't like them. The fact is ferrets can't digest milk products properly. So if you give your pet ice cream, milk, yogurt, pudding, or cheese, he could vomit, get diarrhea, or both. The odd little lick won't do any harm—and your ferret will love you for it. But if your crafty critter helps himself to the milk in your ten-year-old's leftover breakfast cereal, be prepared for a major cleanup.

Many fuzzies love nuts, sunflower seeds, and raisins. When given whole, these can lodge in ferret throats or intestines. Chop them into small pieces to avoid an emergency trip to the veterinarian. Stay away from sticky stuff altogether—peanut butter, marshmallows, gumdrops, and gummy bears can stick in a ferret's throat and cause choking.

Although ferret owners in some countries feed their ferrets fresh chicken, liver, tripe, and all manner of raw meat, in North America this is not a common practice. Raw meat might contain bacteria that could make your ferret sick. The same goes for raw eggs; many ferrets love fresh egg yolks, but the possibility of Salmonella poisoning is too great to take a chance.

These people foods should be on the ferret no-no list.

Chapter Five

Handling

Bringing Your Ferret Home

U nless you're buying a kit directly from a breeder, your new pet has probably made several journeys and had several stopovers in her short life. A kit will often go from a large commercial breeder to a distributor by truck or plane before traveling on to a pet shop. She may or may not be kept together with her littermates, and she certainly won't be with her mama. An adult at a shelter has had at least two moves in her life already and quite possibly more. So when it comes your turn to take a ferret under your wing, start out on the right foot. Pay attention to how you bring her home so that her homecoming is as stress free as possible.

First of all, when you're making arrangements to pick up your pet, choose a time when there's nothing else on the agenda. Don't try to squeeze in the pickup between work and the kid's swimming lessons—this will elevate everybody's stress levels. When you get to the pet shop, breeder, or shelter, don't hurry things. Visit with the new family member for a bit before leaving for the journey home.

On the way home, it's not a good idea to let someone hold the new pet—ferrets can be squirmy, and a ferret on the loose in a car is a recipe for disaster. On the other hand, it's not a good plan to pop the new pet into one of those tiny cardboard boxes that pet stores provide for animal transport. Better bring your own critter carrier. If you bought your pet down at the local mall, a small travel carrier will do, as long as there's room for a litter box. If, on the other hand, you bought her from a breeder or shelter in the next state, take along a large travel cage complete with litter box, food, water, and a cozy blanket for her to curl up in.

Listening to the radio on the ride home is OK, but the new family member won't appreciate rockin' and rappin' with the bass booming in her ears. Stick to something low-key and soothing. Better yet, switch off the music and speak softly to her so bonding can begin. Have the kids come along for the pickup? Don't let them stick their fingers through the travel carrier door—kits sometimes nip when they're frightened and the resulting shriek (kid's? kit's?) could have you driving off the road.

When you get to your house, what's the first thing that will happen? The kids will be clamoring to get the ferret out to play. Everybody will want to hold her, kiss her, and chase her around the floor. Resist these natural impulses—you must put the ferret's needs first. She's in a new place—again—and has to have time to settle in. So take the carrier right over to her cage, carefully transfer her from carrier to cage, then close the cage door, and keep it closed for awhile. Don't let 50 neighbor kids come over to mill around and gawk at her, and *never* allow little fingers to poke at her through the wires. Peace and quiet is the best way to go until the newcomer (a.k.a. the newbie) feels at home in her new surroundings.

Keep your critter close in a comfy carry bag.

Don't be alarmed, however, if the recent arrival shatters the silence herself. Some ferrets, when put into a new cage, will scratch frantically trying to get out. If you get her out right away, she'll learn that scratching equals freedom. So let her scratch. After a while, she'll give up and start investigating the contents of the cage—the food, the water, the litter box, the toys, and the cozy bedding that you put there earlier. When she's had a good snoop around, she'll probably hit the sleepy sack, worn out with all the excitement of the day.

Handling How-To

When the newbie's had a good long snooze, it's time to start getting acquainted. There's a right way and a wrong way to do this. The wrong way is just to grab her right out of the cage and have the whole family crowding in on her. The right way is to sit at the cage and let her get a good look at you. Talk quietly to the new pet; let her get used to your voice while you wait for her to visit the litter box. Then, open the cage door, and while softly repeating her name, reach in confidently and gently pick her up. Cradle her with both hands, one hand supporting her hips and the other her upper body. For added support, cuddle her against you.

If the ferret you've brought home seems stiff and standoffish when held, she's probably frightened.

Chances are she hasn't had enough socializing to feel comfortable with people. Stroke her gently, massage the back of her head, between her shoulder blades and on down her spine. Speak to her in a soft, low-toned voice; this will have a calming effect on her. Another trick to relax that stiff little gal is to massage the top of her front paws with your thumbs. Kneading those front knuckles will often totally relax a ferret. Or how about offering the newcomer a few drops of coat supplement on a plastic spoon? This will help get the right message across—being held is a rewarding experience.

Keep the first handling session short unless you have a snuggle bug that can't get enough of being held. If you have a kit that's willing to be held, by all means, hold her! If you have one that wants to run around and play, then read Chapter 6 to make sure she can play safely.

Cradling your furball against your body helps her feel secure.

The More Often, the Better

When it comes to bonding, you can't handle your fuzzy often enough. The more often you hold and play with a ferret, the better pet she'll be. A pet that's not held won't learn social skills and could even become quite unmanageable.

So, morning, noon, and night, and anytime in-between, find time for that ferret. And if you don't have time, make time. After all, you do want her to be the best pet she can be, don't you? If you're at work or school all day, schedule bonding time before you go out the door in the morning and as soon as you get home at night.

A great way to bond when you're busy is to pop your pet into a carry bag (see Chapter 11) and cart her around the house with you. This way, you'll have your hands free to wash the dishes, surf the Net, do homework, or tidy up, and all the while you can talk to the newcomer, pet her, and slip her the odd treat. Whether the newbie's a kit or an adult, this closeness to you will give her a sense of security and will help her to trust you more quickly.

Does this seem like a lot of work? Keep in mind that the extra time you spend getting to know your ferret in the first few weeks will really pay off down the road. Ferrets flourish when they're given affection.

Is Your Kit Uncooperative?

A lot of kits will lap up attention and snuggle right up to you, but watch for the freedom fighters. As soon as you pick them up, they'll be struggling to get down. And struggling. And struggling. If you have a wiggle worm in your hands, whatever you do, don't let her down right away. Why not? You don't want her to learn that wild wiggling will get her what she wants . . . down. You need to establish that you're the boss—numero uno in the pecking order. Otherwise, that little kit will be ruling the roost in no time. So when she struggles, hang on to her firmly but gently, for a few minutes—then let her down. This way *you're* the one making the decisions, not her.

Of course, it's not the easiest thing in the world to hold a squirming kit. If you're afraid of dropping a fidgety ferret, sit down on the sofa or, better yet, on the floor. And while you're sitting there, why not treat her to a tasty tidbit? That will keep her calm for a minute or two anyway.

However, if the rowdy little rascal is totally out of control, put her back into the cage for a time out. This will give both of you a breather, and you can get her out again later. One thing to keep in mind, though—a really wiggly ferret could be a ferret needing the litter box. Quick . . . get her into the cage. When a ferret's gotta go, a ferret's gotta go.

Make Handling a Family Affair

Have you bought a ferret as a family pet? Then make handling a family affair. The new pet has to get to know everybody in the family but not necessarily all at once in a bunch. What you don't want is to have the kids and all of their friends grabbing at and fighting over one poor, petrified ferret.

"Dad! Make Clare give Fresca to me now."

"That's not fair. Andrew had a longer turn than I did!"

"No I didn't! You had a longer turn last time."

"Gimme that ferret. She's really mine, you know!"

If this is the scene at your house, then you're doing things the wrong way. The right way is to forgo the family politics and put the ferret first. And that means managed introductions with an adult supervisor in control.

Introductions will be different depending upon the age of the

Make ferret care a family affair.

children in your house. Here's the game plan for a young child. Wait until the ferret is tired out or at least quieted down. Sit Sally on the sofa, and place the ferret on her lap. Now show Sally how to hold the new arrival properly, how to pet her, and how to speak kindly to her. Offering the furball a treat will speed up the bonding process. But make sure Sally offers it on a plastic spoon— kits can't always distinguish little fingers from food. Keep the first few sessions short, until kit and kid are well acquainted.

If your pet is a rambunctious kit who prefers running around to cuddling close, it might be a lot easier for Sally to hold a sleeping fuzzy rather than a squirming fuzzy. When ferrets sleep, they're dead to the world, so it would be easy to trans-

fer a snoozing kit to Sally's lap without waking the kit. This game plan encourages closeness and avoids the frustration that could develop if a child wants to hold a kit that doesn't want to be held.

Orchestrating introductions for older children takes planning, too. How you go about it depends upon the child's personality and the ferret's personality. Is your child easy-going and responsible? Or is she hyperactive and a bit flighty? Is your ferret a docile darling or a hopping hellion? Evaluate both person and pet before plotting out the best plan of action. More responsible older children could handle and care for a mild-mannered ferret from the get-go. Whereas pairing a fidgety ferret with a capricious kid could spell trouble . . . a ferret can't take rough handling and is very vulnerable to injury. You're the one who will have to decide when your child is responsible enough to fraternize with the ferret without adult supervision.

Every household has to establish ground rules about the ferret. Here's a commonsense list of ferret dos and don'ts:

• *Do* treat your ferret with kindness and respect—*always*.
• *Do* insist on adult supervision for young children whenever the ferret is out of her cage.
• *Do* teach everyone in the family the correct way to hold and pet a ferret.
• *Do* approach your ferret slowly so you don't frighten her.
• *Don't* mishandle your ferret—no squeezing, no throttling, no tail pulling, no rough stuff. A ferret can easily be injured if mishandled.
• *Don't* poke fingers into your pet's cage.
• *Don't* chase or tease your ferret.
• *Don't* let a new ferret near your face (see next section).

Set up a few sensible rules, stick with them, and the new pet will become a bona fide family member in no time. The goal is for the ferret to bond to the family and for the family to bond to the ferret.

Do You Have a Little Nipper?

New ferret owners need to know that some kits go through a nippy stage just as some kittens and puppies do. Although most kits will "mouth" their owners' fingers, some take this a bit further and actually nab their owners with a nip or two (or three or four). The web of skin between thumb and forefinger seems to be a favorite target spot— and it hurts. Why do kits behave like this?

The most obvious reason is that they're teething and trying out those new teeth. Another possible reason is separation anxiety. After weeks of bonding closely with their mother and littermates, kits suddenly find themselves in a strange environment with no familiar ferret faces around them. Is it any wonder that some of them exhibit signs of stress and nip as a result? If you have an only ferret that could be suffering from separation anxiety, cuddle her, cuddle her, cuddle her. Cart her around in a carry bag as much as possible so that she bonds to you now. When you can't be with her, provide her with a surrogate friend. Ferret-shaped stuffed toys give her something to snuggle up to, and a ticking clock close to the cage will mimic mama's heartbeat. Or, you could buy another ferret!

Other kits aren't suffering from separation stress—they're just plain rowdy. They're still exhibiting the play behavior they learned in the rough-and-tumble of litter life. Baby ferrets have tough skins. From the time they're old enough to walk, littermates will swat at, pounce on, bite at, drag around, and generally beat up on one another. To them, it's all great fun. And they'll try to include their new humans in the fun, too. The problem is, human skin isn't as tough as ferret skin.

You, yourself, might be the unwitting cause of ferret nips. Many ferrets like the smell and taste of soaps and hand lotions. Are your hands a target for ferret teeth? Try using unscented soaps and lotions, and never use them just before handling time. Or, try dipping your hands into a vinegar rinse to neutralize any scent.

If you do have a little nipper, you have to teach her not to nip. In fact, even mild "mouthing" should be discouraged from day one. How do you get this message across? First try holding your kit directly in front of you, look her straight in the eye, and say "No!" in a firm, decisive voice. Do this every time she mouths or nips. At the same time, redirect her teething attempts to something suitable like a Cheweasel or a Super Chew Ferret Toy. These chew toys have a rubbery texture that most ferrets can't resist, but they are safe and digestible, unlike real rub-

ber. A ferret chew bone is another substitute teething ring, but it won't get the rave reviews that the Cheweasels get.

Does saying "No!" make no impression? Then bring out the Bitter Apple, the Bitter Lemon, or the Bitter Lime spray. These bitter sprays are nontoxic, but just one taste will have most ferrets spitting and sputtering. To be effective, spritz the spray liberally all over your hands and wrists. Then, if the nipper pecks your pinkie or nabs your knuckle, she'll get a shock to her taste buds. She'll soon learn that fingers taste terrible. Although these sprays work wonders against most feisty ferrets that are into nibbling fingers, they don't deter all furballs. Ferrets have pretty peculiar tastes, and some actually *like* this stuff.

Did you strike out with the sprays? Is there any other way to nip nipping in the bud? Try rubbing cheap vinegar onto your hands—some ferrets hate the taste. No go? Then take a hint from mama ferret herself—scruffing is her method of keeping the kits in line. Whenever your naughty girl nips or nabs, launch into your Mama Ferret routine. Scruff the scoundrel. Take firm hold of the loose skin on the back of her neck, and lift her up carefully so that her front feet are dangling. Then, while she's hanging helpless with nothing to do but listen, say a loud, convinc-

Redirect a nipper's attention to a ferret chew toy.

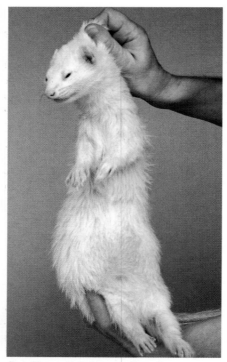

Scruffing mimics mama ferret's disciplinary tactics.

nips, voice your disapproval, "No!" Then whisk her into her cage—do not pass go, do not collect the Ferretone, go straight to jail. Solitary confinement should last about 10 minutes before the games begin again. This loss of freedom is particularly effective if you have another ferret or two cavorting outside the cage, thumbing their noses at the detainee.

Here's something else to keep in mind if you have a nipper on your hands. A ferret with a full meal in her tummy is less likely to mistake your fingers for hot dogs. So always wait until the critter has eaten before you get her out for handling.

Nix the Toe Nipping

No matter how young or old your ferret is or how well trained, human toes are an irresistible temptation. Ferrets love to chase them, pounce on them, and nip them. Why is it that ferrets have a love affair with toes? Do bare toes look like wiggling kits to play with? Are they being mistaken for tasty wieners? Or does that alluring Eau de Toe prompt the toe attacks? Who knows? But the facts speak for themselves. Whether bare or sock covered, toes tempt even the most mild-mannered ferrets.

To prevent sneak attacks on tender tootsies, arm yourself with a bitter spray and mist both feet, from big toe to ankle. A mouthful of spray-spritzed sock will have the toe attacker backing off in a hurry. When

ing "No!" Or mimic Mama's scruff-and-hiss method. Scruff the nipper—being careful not to be rough—and hiss loudly at her.

It goes without saying—but here it is anyway—you must never hurt your ferret when you're correcting her behavior. Discipline is *never* a license to get rough with a pet.

Time-outs are also worth a try. A bouncing baby isn't going to be happy if her playtime's cut short. Although there are no double-blind studies to prove their effectiveness, many ferret owners swear by time-outs. Whenever your wired weasel it comes to toe nipping, ferrets don't discriminate between family and friends. Your toes, your best friend's toes, the Avon lady's toes—your pet's not particular. So when guests ring the doorbell, greet them with a big "Hello!" and a blast of Bitter Apple to the feet. This will certainly get the conversational ball rolling!

Another tactic to deter toe nippers is to encase those feet in thick, bootie-type slippers. These won't necessarily prevent toe attacks, but they will prevent ooches and ouches.

A word of advice—it's not unknown for some family members to enjoy a game of footsies just as much as your ferret does. If you catch Gary wiggling his toes under Fresca's nose, clamp down on him right away before Fresca beats you to it. It's important to put a stop to *all* toe teasing, otherwise your ferret will get confused. How will she know when toe tag's tolerated and when it's taboo?

Deliberate toe teasing is definitely out, but did you know that you could be tempting your pet unwittingly? For some reason, pantyhose act like a magnet to ferrets. Even ferrets that don't usually have a foot fetish have a hard time resisting legs and toes in pantyhose. Using the bitter sprays will often work, but be prepared for plenty of snags and shreds while your fuzzy's learning. You don't have shares in a pantyhose factory? Then pull on long socks, or socks and leg warmers, to protect those exposed hose. Or, get in the habit of hauling on the pantyhose just before you run out the door.

Rehabilitating a Problem Ferret

Do you have a nippy kit? Don't despair. Most kits grow out of this stage by the time they're six months old. This is especially true if your kit comes from a reputable breeder and if she was frequently handled and socialized before you bought her.

There are, however, some ferrets that continue to be nippers well after the nippy stage should be over. What's the reason for this? Some-

Toe nipping needs to be nipped in the bud.

times it's genetic. Not all cats or dogs—or people for that matter—are gentle and sweet tempered. Why should ferrets be any different? More often, though, nipping continues past the kit stage, not because the kit has a nasty disposition, but because she hasn't been handled enough by the humans in her life. Kits need to be held and cuddled frequently; they need to be socialized from a very young age. A six-month-old juvenile who's still waiting for her people placement, and who hasn't had much human handling, may have learned from her littermates that nipping is the norm. Or, consider a ferret that has a home but is confined to her cage for most of the day—she may be nipping out of sheer frustration or depression. Ferrets are not caged animals. They need lots of exercise time and interaction with their owners. A ferret that's kept cooped up is much more likely to nip.

Why else do ferrets continue to nip? In some cases, unneutered male kits become aggressive when they start to hit sexual maturity. Watch out for hard nipping and biting at this stage. In most instances, neutering will take care of the problem. And anyway, you should always have your pet neutered unless you're planning to use him for breeding purposes.

Sometimes ferrets learn to bite in response to mistreatment. Sadly, not all pets start life with the good home they deserve. Some poor ferrets are neglected or abused and learn early in life to distrust humans. Who can

blame them for nipping or even biting? But if you have opened your heart and your home to a mistreated ferret and it's a biter, then you're in a bit of a predicament. You're not going to want to hold a bitey ferret, but holding it and socializing it are the only ways of civilizing it.

What's the answer here? There can be several answers depending on your personality and the ferret's. Are you timid and afraid of being nipped, or can you tolerate being nabbed? Are you confident in your ability to handle ferrets, or are you a rookie and inexperienced? Is the ferret nipping, hard nipping, or outright biting? Is the ferret somewhat cooperative or not cooperative at all? Here are some practical suggestions for managing a bitey ferret—pick what works for you.

Are you an inexperienced owner with a bitey ferret? You could invest in a good, thick pair of garden gloves. Mist them all over with a bitter spray, and wear them each and every time you pick up your pet. It's also advisable to wear long sleeves and spray them, too. Your goal is to hold the ferret as often as possible so that she starts to trust you. Be nice to her—stroke her, pet her, talk softly to her, give her the odd treat. In other words, treat her as if she's special. You'll be able to tell when she starts to respond—she'll enjoy being held. Then it's time to ditch the gloves and spritz your hands instead with the bitter spray. Keep this up, and over time, if you're consistent and persistent, trust will eventually

A ferret can't nip you when held like this.

be built up and you can toss the spray away.

Some owners don't like gloves to come between themselves and their ferrets. Are you one of these? Then how do you hold you pet without getting nipped? Spray your hands with Bitter Apple, Bitter Lemon, or Bitter Lime, and try to hold the ferret so that her little gnashers can't get at you. Hold her head still so she can't whirl it around and nab you. Put your thumb across the back of the head on one side, your forefinger onto the other side (see photo). With the other hand, stroke the top of her head and massage down her back. This gets her used to being handled . . . being petted feels good. Stroke her and talk to her. If you cart her around in a carry bag so she's close to you, this will speed up the bonding, too. Reinforce her good behavior by giving her treats on a plastic spoon. While she's learning to trust you, it's better to hold her for short periods of time. But hold her often.

When you're rehabilitating a nipper, there are some commonsense rules to follow. Never yell at or hit your pet for nipping. Never shake a forceful finger in her face. This will frighten her and encourage more biting. Never say her name in an angry tone because your ferret shouldn't associate her name with getting in trouble. Never hold a nippy ferret near your face—chin skin and earlobes are favorite targets. And don't let children or timid family members handle the nipper until she's learned to mind her manners.

As long as your ferret is showing any tendency toward nipping, don't let strangers handle her. There have been several cases where ferrets, even with up-to-date rabies shots, have been euthanized after nipping, scratching, or biting someone. Don't let this happen to your pet.

Chapter Six
Ferret Proofing

What Is Ferret Proofing?

Having a ferret cruising around the house is not at all the same as having a cat or a dog running around the house. When it's out-of-the-cage time, you won't find your ferret heading for the nearest sunny window ledge for a cat nap or sitting on your knee like a lap dog. Instead, your little live wire will be off and running as soon as he's clear of that cage.

Ferrets are natural-born investigators. You won't believe what they can get into. If left to his own devices, your super sleuth will ferret out every nook and cranny in your house—snoop, snoop, snoop. And he's not going to snoop halfheartedly. Oh, no! He'll put his whole heart and body into it. And what a long, slinky body he has . . . just right for squeezing into the smallest and darkest of spaces, for getting into, under, behind, through, between, and over just about anything.

On top of this, ferrets have pretty weird taste buds. When compared with other pets, they have very

bizarre notions about what appeals to the palate. The average cat doesn't smack his lips over Lysol, but ferrets do. The average dog isn't ravenous for rubber, but ferrets are. Unfortunately, ferrets don't know what's bad for them. They'll happily gobble down all sorts of oddball items that can make them sick, poison them, or cause intestinal obstructions.

So, in view of their excessive curiosity and their unorthodox appetites, ferrets can't be let loose in the house without some advance preparations. And that's what ferret proofing is. It's you as an owner taking the time to make your ferret's play space safe *before* letting the investigator out to snoop. It's getting down to ferret level and looking at each room from a ferret's point of view. Pretend you're a ferret—"What can I get into? Oh, look! There's a plant on the bookshelf! How can I reach it? Wow, here's a Superball to snack on! Can I squeeze under this sofa for a snooze? They'll never find me here. Ah, ha! Someone's left soap on the shower floor . . . yum, yum!"

Ferret proofing is combing through each room carefully and fer-

The great ferret investigator on the job.

reting out the trouble spots before your ferret does. Don't skimp on the ferret proofing—it's one of the most important things you can do to keep your pet safe and healthy.

Setting Boundaries

Before you launch right into ferret proofing, figure out just how much of the house your ferret's going to roam. After all, there's no point in fixing up the whole house if the ferret-friendly zone is limited to two rooms.

Some people set aside one room as the "ferret room." This is where the cage is located, and this is the designated pet playroom. There are advantages to this arrangement. You have to ferret proof only one room, and it's simpler to make that one room totally safe than it is to tackle the whole house. Litter training is *much* easier. Ferret paraphernalia doesn't find its

way all over the house. And, people paraphernalia that could be ferret unfriendly is less likely to end up in the playroom (or in the ferret).

There are also disadvantages to a one-room play place. If the room is too small, it won't give your ferret enough play space. So if you do go the one-room route, make sure the room is roomy. Also, ferrets like human company, and being stuck in one room is not going to foster family feeling. To be fair to your ferret, you'll have to spend a lot of time in the room with him yourself or else provide your pet with a ferret friend. One of the biggest drawbacks to the one-room restriction, however, is that your furball will eventually realize that there's life beyond the door. And when he does, he'll do his darndest to get a piece of the action. Scritch-scratch, scritch-scratch— you won't be too happy when he starts carpet clawing and door scratching to get out.

Some owners advocate the complete opposite of the one-room playroom. They feel that ferrets should have complete free run in the house—nowhere should be off limits. This works best in small apartments or house trailers where total ferret proofing is possible and practical. But in the majority of households, this isn't very realistic. After all, do you feel confident that you can ferret proof every square inch of your whole home?

Most owners take the middle ground. They let their ferrets run part of the house and keep other parts off limits. If you take this route, your ferret will have plenty of space to stretch his legs in safety, but you can keep him out of those spots that are too big of a job or plain impossible to ferret proof.

And how do you keep you ferret out of the trouble spots? The easiest way, when possible, is to close the doors. But what if your doorways don't have doors? Or, what if careless family members keep forgetting to close the doors? Then it's time to buy or make a ferret gate. Buying a gate is easier but more expensive. The only one made specifically for ferrets is a Weezl Watchr ferret gate. Where can you find one? Inquire at your local pet store, or access the Internet. This clear, bendable plastic gate snaps tightly into doorways. It's low enough to step over but high enough to keep all but the most determined high jumpers on the approved side of the gate.

Are you a do-it-yourselfer? It's a cinch to fix up your own ferret gate. Nail up two narrow strips of wood to make a track on the right inside door frame. Do the same on the left. Cut a piece of Plexiglas or Lucite 2 feet (60 cm) high and the width of your doorway, slide it into the tracks, and there you have it—an instant furball barrier. Ferrets like to see what's on the other side of the door, so pass up plywood even though it's cheap and splurge on Plexiglas. And don't waste your money on a baby gate; most ferrets soon figure out how to climb them.

Now it's time to get down to the ins and outs (and the ups and downs) of ferret proofing. The following sections point out the dangers your ferret can encounter in your home. They also outline a variety of solutions or quick fixes to help you make your ferret's play space safe. Before you have a cardiac arrest at the long list of trouble spots, it helps to know that different ferrets have different personalities—they won't all get into, go after, or gobble up the same things. Similarly, not every solution will work for every ferret—that's why several solutions are mentioned wherever possible.

Rubber, Foam, Latex, and Sponge

Ferrets may have different personalities, but the one thing they all agree on is that rubber, foam, latex, and sponge are absolutely delicious. When it comes to this stuff, it's as if they have built-in radar or some type of sixth sense that can lead them right to it. Then watch out! Your ferret's not going to play with the rubber, he's going to eat it. WARNING! Ingested rubber, foam, latex, and sponge can kill. Ferrets often chew off and swallow chunks that are too large to pass through their narrow intestines. Because these materials can't be digested, they either stay lodged in the ferret's stomach or cause a blockage in the intestines themselves. Many a ferret has had to have emergency surgery after going on a rubber binge.

Make sure your fuzzy doesn't become another statistic. Round up all rubber items, and put them out of ferret reach. Look for rubber gloves, rubber-backed throw rugs, boots, runners, rubber sandals, flip flops, slippers, sink or tub plugs, door stoppers, or pencils with erasers on the end. Then find the foam. It will usually appear in the form of foam shoe insoles, pipe insulation, stuffed animal stuffing, Styrofoam cups or plates, pop or beer can cool-

ers, Styrofoam packaging pellets, or the molded Styrofoam that's found as protective padding in boxes.

Latex items such as balloons, cleaning gloves, isometric exercise bands, and condoms need to be kept out of range. So do sponge items such as mop heads (store them sponge side up) and bath and cleaning sponges.

This point can't be too strongly stressed—rubber, foam, latex, and sponge can kill. Keep them away from your furball.

Cabinets and Cupboards

Ferrets are tireless explorers. And did you know that these curious critters have the uncanny knack of getting into cupboards? Indeed, the ferret body seems custom-made for just this purpose. First, ferrets have prehensile paws that can pry open cupboard doors or drawers in a flash. Second, they have long, sinuous bodies that can slither into any gaps between kickboard and cabinet. And when the ferret burglar breaks in, nothing in the cupboard is safe, and

WARNING! Rubber, sponge, latex, and foam are hazardous to a ferret's health! NEVER let your fuzzy near them.

neither is he. Think of the accidents waiting to happen to a free-roving ferret with access to bleach, cleaners, insecticides, ant or rat poisons, plant fertilizers, mouse traps, roach traps, sponges, soap, or shampoos.

There are two ways to get around this problem. One way is to ferret proof the inside of the cupboards. This means removing all ferret-unfriendly items or storing them inside plastic storage boxes with tight-fitting lids. It also means blocking up any gaps around plumbing pipes with ready-mix wall compound before your wiggle worm disappears down inside the walls.

Another way to ferret proof the cabinets is to install baby locks on the doors and drawers. However, not all locks that keep out babies will keep out ferrets. Some baby locks let the doors or drawers open wide enough for a resourceful ferret to wriggle in. A resourceful owner, though, can make a few modifications so that the doors won't open up too wide—hot glue small wooden blocks to the inside of the frame where the latches catch so that the latches hook onto the block rather than onto the frame itself. If you can't be bothered making modifications, magnetic Tot Loks are the answer.

Besides getting into cupboards, ferret explorers can sometimes find ways to get under cupboards. Get down on your knees in the kitchen and bathroom. If there's a space between the kickboard and the cabinets that is larger than 1 inch (2.5

cm), it won't be long before your sneak thief creeps in to investigate. Thwart his efforts. Tack up a piece of wood molding to cover the space, or install a wider kickboard.

One last cupboard check—remove any little rubber bumpers on the inside of the door panels. They're easy for you to overlook, but your rubber hog will find them in no time.

Appliances

Is your ferret going to be allowed into the kitchen? Unless you're planning to tie him to your apron strings, better plan on ferret proofing. Otherwise, while you're cooking up supper, he'll be cooking up mischief. While you're stirring things on top of the stove, he'll be stirring things up behind the stove, under the stove, and in the stove drawer.

Here's a list of the kitchen chores you'd better take care of before your four-footed friend is allowed on KP duty. Block up any space between the stove and the kitchen cabinet by cutting and folding a sturdy cardboard box and wedging it in tightly. To close up the opening between the stove and the floor, twist the stove's adjustable legs so that it sits closer to the floor. To keep the drawer off limits, shove a wooden wedge underneath, or tape it shut with duct tape. If your ferret is a tape ripper, ferret proof the drawer's contents instead of the drawer itself.

Refrigerators pose special problems. Some are virtual fortresses that your marauder can't penetrate. Others are death traps with fans, motors, coils, and insulation all accessible. It's up to you to evaluate your own particular model and block off any openings with heavy cardboard, tape, chicken wire, masonry board, wire mesh screening, or a combination of any of the above. You might also need to tape the front kick plate panel to the sides so that your ferret can't flip it off and crawl underneath—just be careful not to overdo the tape or you could interfere with the fridge's ventilation. Take care, too, when you're getting your bedtime snack out of the fridge—your ferret might be nosing in for a look-see. Don't let the door bonk him in the back, and don't shut him in accidentally.

The dishwasher is for washing dishes, not ferrets. When you're stacking or unloading the dishes, make sure your pet doesn't sneak in the minute your back's turned. With built-ins, block up any gaps next to the cabinet; with portables, don't let any rubber hoses dangle down.

It's difficult to make washers and dryers safe. The best solution is to make the laundry off limits. If this isn't possible, what can you do? Tackle the dryer first. Most dryers are an enclosed box, so the only problem area is the vent hose. Your ferret can chew through the flexible plastic tubing and escape to the great outdoors or into the great dryer insides. Foil his efforts by replacing plastic hose with rigid or flexible aluminum venting. The

A stove drawer is no place for a furball.

washer's more of a headache. Most don't have an enclosed bottom or back, so there's nothing to prevent your pet from vanishing up inside and nibbling drive belts, getting zapped by the motor, getting injured when the machine's turned on, or climbing into the tub and being agitated with the wash. To keep fuzzies from creeping underneath, lower the legs so that the washer is sitting very close to the floor. To keep fuzzies out of the back, either block off all access to the back, or cover any holes with wire mesh screening anchored firmly with several rows of duct tape. Rub the tape well to secure it in place.

Hmmm . . . this looks interesting!

Whenever you're putting in a load of wash, always sift through it first in case a zonked out ferret is snoozing among the socks. Ferrets are not machine washable.

Furniture

Ferrets like to cruise across furniture—sofas, chairs, footstools, tables. If they can climb right onto a table, they will. If they can't get there directly, they're clever enough to work out a roundabout route—from the footstool to the chair, from the chair to the sofa, from the sofa to the table. So if you have knick-knacks, magazines, coffee cups, framed photos, or other essentials crowding those tabletops, better

relocate them before your cruising critter starts knocking them off one by one.

Ferrets like to hide and snooze in dark places. What better place to park than behind, under, or between the cushions of your sofa or chairs? When there's a ferret in the house, never plop down on the sofa for some R & R until you're certain a dozing ferret isn't under the cushion. There's also the underside of the sofa to consider. It's easy for your pet to peel back a corner of the gauzy covering and squeeze right in. Problem is, he could get caught in the springs, he could suffocate, or he could eat the foam stuffing. If your ferret's making a habit of disappearing under the sofa, get down on your knees and take a good look. What's he's up to? Are there any signs of entry or exit holes? Then you'd better upend the sofa and cover the bottom with small-holed chicken wire (nailed in place with fence staples) or with a piece of thin masonite or pressboard (nailed to the frame). Or, if your furniture's seen better days, you could just unscrew the legs and let the sofa sit directly on the floor.

After you've checked under the sofa, go check under the bed, too. The underside of box springs are covered with the same gauzy material that covers the underside of sofas. And guess what? Box springs are also a favorite ferret hideout. If your buddy's making his bed in your boxsprings, the sofa solutions will work for the bed—just get his stash out first.

A sofa bed can be a real pain in the neck. When your super snoop discovers he can worm his way underneath, he'll quickly make it his personal hangout. And just try getting him out of a sofa bed once he's hunkered down in that cozy mattress! Unfortunately, he could suffocate in there, get sat on, or get tangled up in the works. To keep your fuzzball safe, you must keep him out of there. How? Open up the bed and line the inside of the sofa frame with 2-inch × 4-inch (5 cm × 10 cm) wood cut to fit. When the bed is folded up again, the wood is pressed against the sofa frame, creating an effective ferret barrier. For some sofa beds, rolled up chicken wire wedged around the frame might work better. If there are any gaps where wood or chicken wire won't work, jam in stiff cardboard. Ferret proofing a sofa bed is one of those jobs that needs to be done *before* your pet has a chance to get under it. If he once finds his way in and then you block off his access, you'll have one frustrated ferret on your hands. And a ferret never forgets. Months later, he'll still be clawing at the carpet trying to get in. After all, how dare you bar him from his favorite bunk!

Reclining chairs are one of the biggest household hazards where ferrets are concerned. Danger! Danger! Out of sight is often out of mind. Ferrets can sneak into the chair innards and fall fast asleep. Then, when an unsuspecting family member sits back and puts his feet up, the lazy bones under the La-Z-Boy could be crushed in the mechanism. Many a ferret has been seriously injured or has died this way. Don't let this happen to yours. Make this one of the first jobs on your ferret-proofing list. Either get rid of the chair, move it to a ferret-free room, or totally disable the mechanisms that operate the footrest and the reclining back. To fix the footrest, remove the side lever if there is one. Then tip the chair over and use strong rope to tie the metal footrest supports to a stationary part of the chair frame. To immobilize the chair back, completely tighten the wing nuts that control the reclining action and, if there are any slide tracks under the chair, place wooden dowels into them. Your goal is to make the reclining chair into a nonreclining chair. Sit in it and check it out. If you're sitting bolt upright, it's mission accomplished. If you can still recline, it's time to call a furniture repairman to do the job right. Even when your chair's been modified, your pet can still creep underneath and up into the innards where springs, foam, and sharp edges are bad news for a nosy ferret. Heavy-duty cardboard or balled-up chicken wire stuffed around the bottom will keep a ferret out.

Rocking chairs and rocking recliners are death traps for ferrets. If you can't stop the rocking action completely with wooden wedges, move these chairs to a ferret-free zone. For your ferret's sake, please don't take the issue of recliners, rockers,

Uh-oh—that ferret's in the dresser drawers again.

and rocking recliners lightly. These chairs can—and do—seriously injure and kill ferrets.

Even when closed, some dresser drawers and desk drawers can be infiltrated by a determined ferret. Watch him slip his claws into the crack between the drawer and the dresser frame and flip the drawer open. Or watch him crawl underneath the dresser and climb up into the drawers from behind. If there's a way to get in, your ferret will find it. This isn't a problem when the drawer contains nothing but socks and underwear. However, it's a big problem when the drawer contains rubber bands and pencil erasers.

You'll have to prevent access. How? If your pet's levering the drawers open, install baby locks. If he's climbing in from behind or underneath, tack a piece of masonite over the access area.

Kid Stuff

Silly putty, Play-Doh, foamy stuff, Superballs, Nerf balls, rubber balls, hacky sacks, balloons, wheels on toy cars, craft foam . . . in kids rooms, the list of ferret-unfriendly items goes on and on. If your kid doesn't know the meaning of "a place for everything, and everything in its place," make his or her room a ferret-free zone.

What kid's stuff doesn't include sports equipment? Hockey pads, soccer shin pads, mouth guards, rubber studs on baseball shoes, rubber lacrosse balls, runners, helmets for any sport (foam, foam, and more foam), shuttlecocks, grips on rackets, swimming goggles, and snorkeling tubes should all be out of bounds to ferrets. And don't think you can stash stuff in a gym bag—ferrets can wrestle a zipper open in record time.

Office Equipment

Be careful—the four-legged office helper won't be on the job helping you. He'll be helping himself to pencil erasers, rubber bands, stick-tack, calculator buttons, all topped off with a mouthful of tasty mouse pad.

The home office is a prime target for a ferret with mischief on his mind. Here he'll make it his business to rifle through files in the filing cabinet, to find rubber nubbies under lamps, to yank on dangling telephone cords, to reprogram the answering machine, to run off with keys, and to mess with the spaghetti junction of electric cords found under every computer desk. So if you're sharing your office space with a ferret coworker, supervise, supervise, supervise.

Health and Beauty

If your ferret gets his paws on your health and beauty products, you can bet your face mask it's good taste and not good looks he's after. Cotton balls, cotton swabs, makeup sponges, foam curlers, and feminine hygiene products tickle many a ferret's taste buds. Most fuzzies will also lick soap, shampoo, aftershave, body lotions, and face creams until they get sick. Keep all of these health and beauty aids out of your ferret's reach. This includes keeping them out of ferret-accessible wastebaskets. One thing you can guarantee, whatever wastebasket your pal can reach, he'll knock over and ransack in a flash. So, remove the wastebasket from ferret range, stick it into a baby-proofed cabinet, or invest in a step-on pedal bin.

Is it time for your weekly spa treatment in the tub? After a good, long soak, don't get so relaxed that you forget to pull the plug. Otherwise, your furball might jump right in and get into hot water—although ferrets can swim, there's a limit to how long they can keep going before going under.

Entertainment Centers

A home entertainment center will entertain the whole family—ferret included. After seeing a few movies popped into the VCR, just watch your pet try popping in himself. Only a small ferret could squeeze all the way in, but don't take any chances. Keep noses, heads, and paws out of the VCR by installing a child lock made for the slot.

High on the ferret hit list are stereo speakers. Rock, classical, jazz, or

Keep kids' rooms ferret free—they're just too hard to ferret proof.

Close up those subwoofer tubes with wire and tape to keep out nosy ferrets and keep the music booming.

punk, it's not the music that will attract your fuzzy friend, it's the foam he smells deep inside the speakers. To get at it, he'll pry off the front panels and rip the insides to shreds. Not only is this a disaster for you and your speakers, it could mean an emergency trip to the vet if your foam fanatic has swallowed any of the shreds. How can you protect your speakers? The easiest solution for small speakers is to put them up out of ferret reach. Floor speakers are more difficult to ferret proof. Check the sound shop for speaker stands—you might find something tall enough. You could also place a Scat Mat or Pet Mat in front of each speaker. These mats have been designed to deter pets from going where you don't want them to go. They plug into an electric outlet and give off an unpleasant static pulse

when stepped on. This won't harm your ferret a bit, but he won't like the sensation and will back off pronto. It's worth the investment to keep your pet safe and to protect expensive speakers. (See Chapter 9 for more information on pet mats.)

Subwoofers are double trouble. Not only can a ferret pop off the front panel, he can get in through the back door, too. Subwoofers have built-in ferret tubes in the back—or, at least, that's what your fuzzy thinks they are. And you can be sure that he'll weasel through at every opportunity and have a heyday inside. You might have to move the subwoofer up out of reach to a less-than-optimum location.

If you're lucky and your pet shows no interest in yanking off the front panel, you could leave the subwoofer at floor level as long as you block off the tube holes in the back. How can you do this and still keep the woofer woofing? Take a piece of galvanized quarter-inch mesh and cut out a circle about one-half inch wider in diameter than the hole. Cut slits into the outside edge of the circle, one-half inch deep and one-half inch apart. Then bend the cut edge up so that the mesh takes on the shape of a jar lid (see photo). Wedge this into the tube with the cut edge facing you. Lastly, anchor the cut edge to the inside of the tube with heavy-duty duct tape. And voilà—your ferret can't get in, but sound can still blast out.

Most multimedia centers have multiple remote controls, and each one has row upon row of little rubber buttons. Every remote is a ferret magnet, and every button is a potential hazard. Ferrets will drag remote controls out of sight and rip off the rubber at their leisure. Move every remote out of ferret range. And while you're at it, store any headphones on a high shelf so that foam earpieces have a chance of surviving intact.

Stereos, surround-sound receivers, televisions, and VCR's all have one thing in common—electric cords. And electric cords can have a shocking or even fatal effect on your furball. Chewing on the lamp cord, or just play tugging on it, could mean an unscheduled visit to the vet. Have you seen your ferret playing with electric cords? Either put the cords up out of reach, or smear them with Bitter Apple cream. Don't waste your time or money threading the cord through pliable plastic aquarium air hose—ferrets like this stuff as much as the cord.

Heating and Cooling Systems

Ferrets and furnaces are not a good mix. It's all too easy for nosy busybodies to crawl into dark openings and get their whiskers (or worse) burned. Then there are the furnace air vents. Burrowing and tunneling are second nature to ferrets—if your ferret can pry up the floor vent covers, he'll have a whole subterranean network of heating ducts to tunnel through. Does your friendly furnace man have a ferret detector? Ductwork is no place for a furball—there are sharp metal screws, dangerous drops, and life-threatening hazards if he reaches the furnace. To make sure he can't vanish into the heating system, secure the vent covers. Either adjust the side tabs to make the covers tight fitting, or screw the covers to the floor. In some older homes, decorative cold air returns can also give a ferret easy access to the duct work. You might have to put galvanized 0.5-inch (1.3 cm) mesh screening across the hole under the vent cover. This lets the cold air in but keeps ferrets out.

Electric baseboard heaters and hot water radiators pose their own problems—they're hot, they're down at ferret level, and they're interesting to investigate. Because they come in different shapes and sizes, there's no one solution to ferret proofing them all. Check yours out carefully, and take appropriate steps to make them safe.

Fans and window air conditioners can also be a concern when there's a ferret in the house. Floor fans sometimes get knocked over; older models can injure poking ferret paws. There's a fast fix for fans— move them out of the way of playful pets. Or, invest in a tall floor-stand model.

A ferret that's showing any interest in a window air conditioner is probably not looking to adjust the temperature—he's after the foam insulation you've stuffed between the unit and the window. How can you foil his efforts? Here are three suggestions. Rearrange the furniture so he no longer has a pathway to the unit. Move the unit to another window that he can't reach. Or, cover the insulation completely with duct tape.

Windows and Doors

For your furry friend, open doors are an open invitation to the great outdoors. While you're saying good-bye to company, your ferret could slip out unnoticed and hightail it to the open road. Impress on everyone in the family the importance of keeping outside doors closed when the ferret's around. A door left even slightly ajar is "open sesame" to a cunning ferret. Sliding doors with an easy-glide action are a cinch for little paws to open. Always lock those sliders. And sliding screen doors are double trouble. Not only can a ferret slide them open, he can tear them open. Ferrets are notorious for scratching through screens. There really isn't a good, practical solution to screen scratching, but here are some suggestions.

The easiest solution is to replace the existing screen with Pet Screen. This heavy-duty screening has been specially designed to prevent pets from scratching their way through. It will foil most ferrets. You can't find Pet Screen or don't like the look of it? Here are a couple more ideas.

For sliding screen doors, first make sure the screen is closed. Next, slide the interior glass door all the way open. Then place a 2-foot-high (60 cm high) piece of Plexiglas or Lucite across the opening, between the door frame and the open glass door. Lastly, close the interior door against the piece of Plexiglas so that the Plexiglas is jammed between the door frame and the glass door. What you've done is fashioned a see-through, step-over barrier between pet and screen.

For hinged screen doors, have a Plexiglas insert made for the bottom half. Or replace the existing door with a pet-proof one—glass at the bottom and screen at the top.

Open windows can be a problem, too, if they're within ferret reach. And don't think a screen will keep your ferret from escaping—he'll just knock it out or scratch his way through. If he's getting to a window via other furniture, move the furniture. But if the window's low down at ferret level, you're in trouble. Keep it closed or replace the existing screen with Pet Screen and install a screen lock. The Pet Screen is hard to scratch through, and the lock prevents your pet from popping the screen out. For double-hung windows, you could put a portable, expandable screen in front of the existing screen. This is often enough to deter ferrets from screen scratching because, with the extra screen in place, there isn't enough window ledge left for a screen scratcher to perch on.

With some types of windows, you can put two or three sturdy tension rods (from the curtain department) right across the front of the window frame, from one side of the frame to the other. This will prevent most ferrets from landing on the ledge and scratching to their hearts' content.

Do you live five floors up? Do you have a beautiful view from your balcony? Don't let your ferret out to enjoy it. Ferrets don't have good depth perception. They don't seem to figure that heights are anything to worry about and will walk off the edge of a balcony without realizing that the ground is a long way off. So guard against free-falling ferrets; keep them off the balcony and they won't become casualties of high-rise syndrome.

Holiday Ferret Proofing

You've done a great job of ferret proofing your house or apartment for everyday living. However, as different holidays roll around, all kinds of once-a-year decorations come out of storage. Although all this new stuff will have your furball jumping for joy, it could cause headaches for you. So is it possible to have a ferret and deck the halls, too? The answer is yes, as long as you're prepared to get down to some special holiday ferret proofing.

Consider Christmas first. Your biggest headache will be the tree.

At Christmas, a Santa suit won't be the only thing your fuzzy's getting into.

Some ferrets climb Christmas trees; others steal ornaments. Some lap up water in the tree stand; others haul away the lights. Some are tinsel thieves; others purloin presents. And, if given half a chance, almost every ferret will tunnel under the tree skirt.

If you have a tree climber (and not all are), the easiest solution is to set up the tree in a ferret-free room. But if you want your ferret to share in the holiday spirit, pick out a smaller tree that can be placed on top of a ferret-proof table. Or, surround a full-sized tree with a circular or semicircular Scat Mat or Pet Mat (see page 87). Be sure to tape the mat down with wide, clear packing tape so that your tireless tunneler can't creep underneath.

A Pet Mat will also prevent your ferret from creeping under the tree skirt, possibly toppling the tree. And, it will keep him away from the water in the tree stand—the preservatives and/or bacteria found there are bad news for ferret tummies. No mat? Then remove the tree skirt, and form galvanized wire screening or small-holed chicken wire into a tree stand cover.

Even if your pet's not interested in climbing to the top of the tree, he'll be able to help himself to anything dangling on the lower branches. Ornaments, tinsel, candy canes, popcorn strings, garlands—won't these look pretty decorating his stash? Unfortunately, they could end up decorating his intestines, and your Christmas Eve could end up with a Christmas visit to the vet. Avoid potential mishaps by leaving the lower tree branches bare.

And this means no bottom-of-the-tree lights, either. Your little Hercules could tug on them and pull the tree over, he could chew or steal decorative covers, or he could bite the cords and either get zapped himself or flambé the tree.

Piles of presents under the tree always look festive, but a ferret can't

Trick or treat!

read the calendar. He won't wait till Christmas morning to attack the wrapping. He'll just wait till your back is turned. Some ferrets will actually eat ribbons, bows, fancy doodads, and gift wrap—not a healthy diet for a safe holiday season. So pile up presents on a ferret-proof table, or keep them out of sight until the big day. And speaking of the big day, when the family's busy opening presents, what are you going to do with the ferret? Why not appoint a designated ferret watcher to keep an eye on the fur-ball and prevent him from making off with packing foam, rubber bands, plastic bags, small presents, and all the other Christmas paraphernalia? But if Christmas morning is too chaotic at your house, it might be best to confine the kleptomaniac to his cage.

Holiday decorating isn't confined to the Christmas tree. What about candles, wreaths, Nativity scenes, Christmas villages, music boxes, and floral arrangements sitting on low tables? What about garlands on stairs and stockings on mantles? And holiday decorating isn't confined to Christmas time. What about Hanukkah with its menorah and dreidels? What about Easter with baskets, flower arrangements, and chocolate candy? What about Halloween with jack-o'-lanterns, rubber masks, face makeup, and candy, candy, candy? What about the Fourth of July with sparklers and firecrackers? What about birthdays with balloons, presents, and candles? Whenever your everyday decor is livened up for a holiday, you'll have to keep a watchful eye out for your ferret.

Holidays often mean company's coming. And guests who aren't used to ferrets can spell disaster. They don't know to watch their step, to look before they sit, to keep their suitcases off the floor (remember, ferrets can open zippers), to keep purses out of ferret reach, and to keep doors to the outside closed. Little visitors can play too roughly with the ferret, and little ferrets can play too roughly with the visitors. When company descends, it may be safer for all concerned to restrict your pet's out-of-the-cage time to times when you can supervise.

Ding-a-ling! You can keep track of your furball when he's wearing a bell on his collar.

Wired for Sound

Now you know all about everyday ferret proofing and all about special-day ferret proofing, but there's one little detail that hasn't been taken care of. And that little detail is your little furball! Ferrets don't make noise when they move. Stop for a minute and close your eyes—a whole herd of ferrets could go running by and you wouldn't hear a sound. Without some sort of warning system, your ferret can flit phantomlike from room to room, from mischief to mischief. A small bell will let you chart his progress and pinpoint his exact location.

There's a decision to make here. Is the bell to hang from a harness or from a collar? Collars are lightweight, inexpensive, and readily available. Just be sure to buy one that has built-in stretch. Then, if your industrious investigator gets hooked or hung up on something when he's playing, he can back out of the collar and get free. But being able to back out of a collar easily can be a drawback—your escape artist can ditch his collar and bell on a regular basis. Better keep a couple of spares in the drawer.

An H harness made for a ferret and fit properly is almost impossible to escape from. Even your mini Houdini won't be able to worm his way out. Another advantage to a harness is that a ferret who gets hooked or hung up on something when he's

Some owners prefer to fit their ferret with an H harness and bell.

playing won't get choked as he could in a collar. Some ferrets do, however, have a little difficulty adjusting to the restriction of a harness. And ferrets that wear a harness for long periods of time risk getting bald spots where the harness rubs.

Whether you opt for a collar or a harness to hold the ferret warning system (ding-a-ling), it's a good idea to remove it when your fuzzy's in his cage. There's no sense in taking a chance of your ferret being hurt, hooked, or hung in his cage. And anyway, when he's in his cage, you know where he is.

Lost and Found

Even with the best ferret proofing, it is possible for some little sneaks to get out of the house or apartment.

Can you make sure that everybody in the family closes every door, every time they come and go?

You need to know that ferrets don't have the homing instinct of cats. A ferret on the loose is unlikely to find his way back to his home base. So if the unthinkable does happen, it's up to you to spring into action immediately and go find him. The moment you realize that your ferret is missing, quickly but thoroughly search the whole house while using his favorite squeaky toy (see Chapter 8). Check all of his favorite sleeping and hiding spots, look in cupboards, under furniture, in and under clothing, and *squeak, squeak, squeak* as you go. Don't forget to check his cage—he might have snuck in there for a quick snooze.

No luck? Then head outside without delay. In fact, if more than one family member is home, one person should be checking outside while the other person is checking inside. Do a quick search and *squeak* of the front and back yards. If that doesn't turn up anything, put your ferret's cage out onto the porch complete with his favorite blanket, fresh food, and water—he might wander back to familiar territory. Then arm yourself with Ferretone and the trusty squeaker, and start combing the neighborhood. Knock on your neighbor's doors and ask for permission to check their yards. Try and enlist their aid as well. Look under decks and porches, in drain pipes and culverts, behind sheds and composters, under bushes and shrubs.

In short, turn the neighborhood upside down.

Perhaps you live in an apartment building rather than a house. Before you head outside, comb the corridors, the stairways, the elevator, the laundry room, and knock on your neighbors' doors. In short, turn the apartment building upside down.

Still no luck? Head for the computer and slap together a lost-and-found poster. Include such details as your ferret's name, color, size, your telephone number and address, and anything else you think relevant. Leave a space for a recent photo. Tape the photo to the poster, have photocopies made, and post these all over your neighborhood. Call your local radio station, put an ad into the local papers, and offer a reward. Ask your letter carrier, newspaper carrier, and ad bag carriers to keep an eye open for your furry friend. Notify the local Humane Society, any nearby ferret club or shelter, and any veterinary offices, and call them back frequently.

Your chances of getting a lost ferret back are greatly increased if he's wearing a collar or harness. This immediately alerts a stranger to the fact that this furry creature he's found is a pet, not a wild animal. Better yet, equip the collar or harness with some sort of ID; attach a tiny identification tag or have the bell engraved with your telephone number. Or, you could have the collar or harness embroidered with a name and phone number. Of course, ID on a collar won't do any good if your ferret slips the collar—remember, harnesses are harder to escape from.

Because ferrets are great escape artists, many veterinarians now recommend that microchips be implanted into them at their first veterinarian visit. These high tech ID chips, no larger than a grain of rice, are painlessly injected under the skin. This is a permanent method of pet identification—there's no way your ferret can lose it. So, if your microchipped ferret ever lands up at a Humane Society or shelter, he can be scanned and quickly reunited with you.

Here's another piece of advice. Soon after you get him, introduce your fuzzy to all the other households in your neighborhood or apartment building. A ferret that's a familiar sight to your neighbors is less likely to wander far before being apprehended and returned home.

Ferrets don't have a homing instinct. If your pet gets lost outdoors, go look for him immediately.

Chapter Seven
Litter Training

Reality Check

If ferret fanciers all across the country were asked, "What's your ferret's biggest behavior problem?" it's a safe bet that the winning answer would be . . . "litter training!" This is probably the one area where nearly all ferret owners run into difficulties. Part of the problem is that new owners often have false assumptions and expectations. Many have been told, "Litter training is easy. You can litter train a ferret just like a cat." And so owners are expecting ferret performance to equal cat performance.

But let's face facts—a ferret is not in the same league as a cat when it comes to litter training. Cats are the pros. They know instinctively how to use a litter pan, they will come to one pan from anywhere in the house, and they almost never have accidents. Ferrets, on the other hand, are the greenhorns. They need to be taught the ins and outs of litter training, they need multiple boxes if they roam the house, and even the best-trained ferret is liable to have the occasional accident.

So before you can do a good job of litter training your ferret, you need to forget the cat comparisons and familiarize yourself with the ferret facts. Read through this chapter—find out what you can and cannot expect from your pet. Then with your expectations firmly founded on ferret performance, follow the training techniques step-by-step for your best bet at success.

What Can You Expect?

You'll be happy to know that your ferret *can* be trained to use a litter box. The question is—how quickly and how completely will he catch on? All ferrets are different. Some are fast learners; some are slow learners. Some will hit that box 100 percent of the time. A rare few will make infrequent visits. But the good news is that most ferrets can learn to use the litter box most of the time.

The success rate is based on a number of different factors. For example, there's the age element. Although you *can* train an older ferret, it's easier to train a kit that hasn't had time to develop bad habits. Then there's the ferret's experience with a box to consider. A kit or adult that's been introduced to a litter pan at the pet shop, shelter, or breeder's will already know what the pan is for.

Other factors can also influence litter box success. For instance, how much time does your ferret spend in his cage? How much of the house does he roam? How large are the rooms he's playing in? How many litter pans are available? How committed are you to the process? A ferret needs to be *trained* to use a box. Are you ready, willing, and able to put in the time and effort needed? Do you have what it takes to be consistent . . . day after day after day? If the answer is yes, then it's on to the next step.

A Look at Litter Boxes

To start off on the right foot, you need to pick the right litter box. And in order to choose the right box, you need to know something about a ferret's latrine habits.

When your furball is ready to do his business, he'll sniff around, back up into a corner, lift his tail, and then relieve himself. If he's in a box with low sides, chances are his droppings will plop overboard and onto the floor. So, to keep his waste in the litter box where it belongs, you'll need to look for a box with high sides.

But a box with four high sides won't do. Ferrets have short legs. Although they don't think twice about

leaping into a houseplant, there's no guarantee they'll leap into a litter box. If it's a pain to get into the pan, they just won't bother. Instead, they'll take the easy way out and back up beside it. This is especially true for kits and for sick or elderly ferrets. Even if your ferret's happy to hurdle repeatedly over a high side, he risks irritating his belly or penis. So make sure the box you buy has one low side or at least a low entryway for safe and easy access.

Ferret Litter Boxes

Your best bet for a ferret litter box is—surprise, surprise—a ferret litter box. Yes, ferret voices have been raised, and manufacturers have

Backing up with tail raised, Patch performs in the pan.

65

Small corner litter pans are ideal for cages.

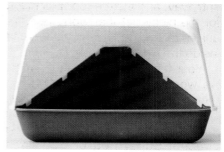

Add a hood for the ferret that likes to do his business in private.

A supersized rectangular box is roomy enough for large ferrets.

listened. They've come up with ferret-specific litter pans in a range of shapes and sizes.

First, there are corner pans. These are triangular, with two high sides that slope down to a low front—the perfect shape for reversing ferret derrieres. Corner pans come in two sizes. The smaller ones are perfect for small cages or travel cages because they're a good fit and can be securely anchored. But don't use them around the house—they tip over too easily.

Super Pet makes a small corner pan that can be fitted with a hood to provide more privacy on the job. Some ferrets will appreciate this private privy; others will mistake it for a canopy bed. It's not a good idea for your ferret to sleep in his litter. So, if he turns his bathroom into a bedroom, hide the hood.

For larger cages and for ferret free-roam zones, the bigger corner pans are better buys. They're unlikely to be tipped over, they have the mandatory high sides and low entryway, and they're roomy enough for the picky pet that won't perform unless all four feet are firmly planted inside the pan.

Your ferret's no geometry genius. He won't insist on triangular pans; rectangular ones will suit just as well. Check out those made by Marshall Pet Products, Inc., Sheppard and Greene, Super Pet, or Suburban Products Incorporated (SPI). They all have three high sides and a low opening at one end, but they vary a bit size-wise. If you're not sure what size to buy, why not take your ferret along on the shopping trip and fit pet to pan?

Cat Boxes

Are cat pans ferret friendly? They can be if the sides are high enough for ferret backups (at least 4 inches (10 cm) high) and the way in is low enough for ferret access. No entryway in sight? No problem. Find a hacksaw, cut out a doorway, then smooth the cut edges with medium-grade sandpaper.

Cat litter boxes with hoods are great for the fastidious ferret that doesn't like to be watched while doing his business. They're also great for fastidious owners because they hide the evidence after the fact. Again, the entryway might have to be modified.

Easy-clean cat boxes are fast becoming the rage for felines. Several types are available—stacked boxes with built-in sifters, roll-over hooded

boxes, even battery operated self-cleaners. But don't get carried away by the novelty. Before you plunk your money down for one of these, make sure it's ferret friendly with high sides and easy access. After all, it doesn't matter that the box is easy to clean if there's nothing in it! And one more point, these boxes can be used only with clumping litters.

Homemade Boxes

Short on cash? Will the cost of multiple boxes break the bank? Then the do-it-yourself litter box is the easy answer. And, you don't need to be a rocket scientist to make one (or many). Take a trip to your local discount store, and buy a plastic storage container or dish pan approximately 14 inches (35 cm) long × 10 inches (25 cm) wide × 7 inches (18 cm) high. Make sure it's made of pliable plastic, not the hard, rigid kind. Then, cut out a section approximately 4 inches (10 cm) × 4 inches (10 cm) from one of the short

A homemade box—inexpensive and easy to make.

Clumping clay for quick cleanup.

ends to provide a low entry. Don't cut down too far—the lower edge of the doorway needs to be at least 2 inches (5 cm) above the floor or the litter will spill out. Finally, smooth the edges with sandpaper and voilà— the perfect ferret litter pan at a penny-pinching price (see photo).

The Scoop on Litter

Choosing a litter box is easy. It's choosing what goes inside the box that's the challenge. If you've strolled down the aisles of your local pet supply store lately, you'll know that there are dozens of different types and brands of litter available. So how do you pick out the best one? Eeney, Meeney, Miney, Moe? Luck of the coupon? Special of the week? The cheaper, the better?

Before you come to any decision, better ferret out the facts. Ideally, what you're looking for is a litter with good odor control that is safe, absorbent, nontracking, readily available, environmentally friendly, and affordable. However, all litters are not created equal, and no one litter is *the* perfect ferret litter. So before you make your choice, read through the next several sections for a review of the leading litters.

Clay Litters

By far, the easiest litter to find is plain old clay cat litter. It's stocked just about everywhere—at the pet store, the grocery store, the discount store, the pharmacy. It comes in small bags, big boxes, and every size in between. And, it's cheap.

Regular clay litter is, however, very dusty. Do you really want to be breathing in silica dust when you're filling up or cleaning out litter boxes? Do you really want your ferret exposed to dust-induced respiratory problems or eye irritation? Younger ferrets often play and tunnel in their litter, and all ferrets stir up dust when going in and out of the pan. So if you opt for regular clay litter, buy the 99 percent dust-free type.

Clumping clay litter is easier to clean up than regular clay litter. You'll really appreciate this if you're on poop patrol and have to clean multiple boxes. A quick scoop or two in each box is all it takes. Just make sure to do the rounds every day because after a few days the clumps break apart when scooped. And also make sure that the litter is at least 2 inches (5 cm) deep, or the urine will percolate through the litter and form cementlike blobs that stick to the bottom of the box.

You might like clumping litter fine, but is it fine for your ferret? The tiny clay particles can cause crusting in nostrils or in anal passages, especially if your ferret is rooting with his nose or dragging his bottom through the litter. The particles can also stick to fur or paws and be licked off and swallowed . . . bad news if they forms clumps inside your ferret. The clay itself can dry out skin, fur, and paw pads.

Meticulous housekeepers won't be big fans of clumping litter because it's terrible for tracking onto carpets. It works its way right down into the fibers and is almost impossible to vacuum out. On hardwood floors, it acts like sandpaper. Newspaper or an old towel under the boxes will protect your floors, but take note—this litter can really fly.

Although clay litter is a natural product, it's neither flushable nor biodegradable. So with landfill sites fast filling up, many responsible owners are switching from clay litters to more environmentally friendly products.

Corncob Litters

If clay's not to your liking, corncob litter is a good environmental choice—it's made from a renewable resource and it's biodegradable. Like clay, it comes in two forms—regular and clumping. Regular crushed corncob, like Clean-N-Comfy or Bed-o' cobs, has reasonable absorbency and odor control. It is, however, extremely light and fluffy—compulsive diggers will have it out of the box and all over the cage in no time. It also tracks easily, but it's a breeze to vacuum.

If you're a fan of clumping litter, why not give clumping corncob (like Clump 'N Flush) a try? You'll love it. It has all the advantages of clumping clay—easy box cleanup, easy litter top-up, and good odor control. In addition, it's virtually dust free and, unlike clay products, the clumps can be flushed. However, if your ferret takes to taste testing the clumping corncob, he could get sick—switch to something else. And remember, if your ferret's a rooter, clumping litter of any kind isn't a good choice.

Regular and clumping corncob litters are environmentally friendly.

Pelleted Paper Products

Paper products are hitting the headlines in the litter lottery. Not your own yesterday's newspaper—which isn't at all absorbent or odor controlling—but pellets made from recycled paper. Look for BioFlush, Marshall Pet Products, Sheppard and Greene, or Yesterday's News.

Some of these products are advertised as being dust free but it's really more accurate to say they're low dust. This low dust factor, combined with the fact that they take a while to break down after absorbing urine, makes paper pellets a great choice for ferret rooters and burrowers. The dust may, however, cause problems for a small percentage of respiratory-sensitive owners.

Pelleted paper is very absorbent, much more so than regular clay litter. Odor control is fairly good. Some brands contain enzymes to counter that familiar ferret fragrance. And for ferret owners with supersensitive noses, Lemon Fresh from Yesterday's News is just that—lemon fresh.

A 1-inch (2.5 cm) layer of paper pellets is all that's needed, making them fairly cost effective. They don't track much, and any pellets that do land on the floor are easily picked up. Litter box cleanup is a breeze. Just scoop out the solid waste on a daily basis, and flush it away. You can get rid of the urine-soaked pellets the same way. Having trouble finding them? Here's a clue: aim for the ones that look more swollen than the rest. And when you're flushing them, never toss more than a scoop at a time down the toilet, or the ferret won't be the only thing backing up in your house.

Pelleted paper litters—nontracking and biodegradable.

Paper pellets are doubly environmentally friendly. The paper they're made from has already been recycled, *and* they're biodegradable. In fact, the pellets break down faster than the newspapers they're made from.

However, biodegradable doesn't mean digestible. Swallowed paper pellets can swell up inside your ferret and cause internal blockage. If your ferret shows any inclination to eat them, *switch to something else.*

Wood Products

In the search for the perfect litter, many ferret owners are turning to wood products. But not just any wood will do. Most pet products made from cedar and pine contain chemicals called phenols that can cause respiratory problems and possible liver damage in small animals. Play it safe; stay away from cedar completely and stay away from pine unless it's been heat treated to remove the phenols. Kiln-dried compressed pine pellets such as All Pet Pine, Feline Pine, or Pine Fresh won't cause health problems for your ferret.

The same goes for phenol-free hardwood products. Try aspen pellets made by the Barnaby Farms Company or by Gentle Touch Products. Both companies make cat litter and small-animal bedding. You might want to use the bedding pellets because they're larger and look less like ferret food. If, however, your

Pine pellets are a good choice, but buy only those brands that have been heat treated to make them phenol free.

ferret does the occasional taste test, don't worry. The pellets quickly break down into tiny particles that won't cause internal blockage. On the other hand, they're not nutritious. So if your pet consistently confuses his litter with his lunch, it's time to switch.

What are the pros of wood pellets? First and foremost, they're supersoakers and top-notch odor eaters. The pellets absorb urine like a sponge. If you scoop the poop daily, a 1-inch (2.5 cm) layer will stay fresh smelling for one to two weeks before needing a complete change.

For superior absorbency and odor control, aspen wood pellets are hard to beat.

This makes them more economical than they might appear at first glance.

Wood pellets are a household-friendly choice because they contain no silica dust, no chemicals, and no deodorizers, and the pellets themselves don't track. They're an environmentally friendly choice because they're made from 100 percent recycled material, they're flushable (in small quantities), and they're biodegradable.

Any cons to wood pellets? The natural, fresh, woodsy smell of aspen pellets can be a pro or a con, depending on who's smelling it. For some people, it's a plus; others may find it too much of a good thing. If you're fragrance intolerant, sniff before you buy. Another possible drawback is that the pellets break down into sawdust as they soak up urine. Kits and ferrets that like to root or sleep in the litter box might get a nose full. And, the sawdust does track.

Do you have lots of ferrets and lots of litter boxes? Are you watching your budget? Then here's a great suggestion. Hardwood wood-stove pellets make an inexpensive alternative to packaged wood litter. Many breeders and multiferret families are choosing these because they're *cheap*—small bucks will get you a big bag. And they have the superior absorbency and excellent odor control of the aspen and kiln-dried pine pellets. However, if you live in Miami rather than Montana, you might have trouble finding them.

You've probably seen wood shavings used as ferret litter because they're cheap and easy to find. But don't be talked into using them. They don't do nearly the same job as wood pellets. Not only will the litter pans stay wet and smelly, you'll find shavings all over your floor. And most importantly, cedar and untreated pine shavings aren't safe for your ferret.

Grain- and Grass-Based Products

In the great litter debate, grain- and grass-based products are popping up as possibilities. Clumping wheat, for example, is an all-natural crushed wheat product that has all the cleanup advantages of clumping clay, plus it's flushable and biodegradable. Heartland Wheat Litter and Swheat scoop are names to look for.

Clumping wheat, like clumping clay, is dusty. The difference is in the

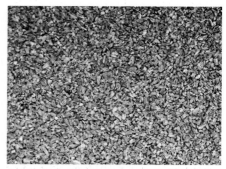

Clumping wheat litter—all-natural and flushable.

If you like pelleted litters, try the grain-based products—they're an excellent option.

type of dust—with wheat there's no silica to worry about. And you'll probably notice the dust only when you're transferring the litter from package to pan or when scooping waste. So pour slowly and scoop gently to avoid billowing dust. Although this litter might not be a good choice for tunneling ferrets (cough, wheeze, snort, sneeze), it's a good option for ferrets that eat pelleted products.

How is clumping wheat in the tracking department? The particles, being small and light, do track. This might not be a hassle for a one-ferret family, but it could be a housekeeping headache for a multiferret family.

Grain-based litters also come in pelleted form, such as Critter Country, made from red winter wheat grass, or Cat Works, made from grain by-products. Both types have excellent absorbency and odor control, they're flushable and biodegradable, nondusty, and nontracking. As with wood pellets, the solid waste should be scooped daily, and the complete contents of the box replaced every week or two.

Remember, some ferrets eat pelleted litter. If yours occasionally munches on Cat Works, you needn't run to the vet because it rapidly breaks down into tiny particles that are digestible. Critter Country, on the other hand, takes longer to break down, so don't let your ferret eat it.

One litter you won't have any trouble finding is alfalfa pellets . . . a.k.a. good old rabbit food. It's environmentally friendly, nontracking, available in bulk, and really cheap. However, it leaves a bit to be desired in the absorption and odor control departments.

Switching?

Trial and error is the name of the game when you're looking for a litter that gets the two thumbs-up rating from you and the four-paws seal of approval from your ferret. But when you've hit on the right product, stick with it. Don't switch with every new special at the pet store, or your confused ferret might boycott the box.

However, what if you need to change litters—perhaps for health or safety reasons, perhaps because a superior product appears on the market? Will your ferret cooperate? The answer is maybe, maybe not. If your ferret falls into the maybe not category, here's what to do. Put a layer of new litter into the pan, and cover it with a layer of the old stuff. Gradually increase the amount of new litter and decrease the amount of the familiar stuff until you have made a complete changeover. During the switch, keep a close eye on your ferret in case problems arise. If your furball starts to munch, sneeze, or itch—switch!

The litter pan should be located in a corner of the cage.

Cage Training

You've picked the pan, you've poured in the litter, now it's time to get down to training. The cage is the obvious and also the easiest place to start—your ferret's in a confined space and can focus better on the job at hand.

Because ferrets prefer to drop their little loads in corners, the first step is to choose a corner in the cage for the litter pan. The next step is to anchor the pan in place. Why? Most ferrets are compulsive furniture rearrangers—watch that litter fly as they heave and hoe the box to another spot. Others are plain mischievous and will move the box out of the way so they can go in the corner itself. The easiest way to keep the pan in place is to use universal cage clips made for this very purpose by Super Pet (see photo). Can't get your hands on any? You can always try the hot-nail trick. Hold a nail with a pair of pliers, heat up the nail over the stove or with a match, and poke a hole (or two) through the litter box. Then, take a piece of wire, a long twist tie, or a metal shower curtain hook, thread it through the hole, and attach it to the cage wire. This will foil your ferret's furniture-moving activities, and you'll be able to remove the pan for easy cleaning.

When the pan's in place, watch your ferret's reaction. Will he use it for its intended purpose? Many ferrets already familiar with a litter box at a pet store, shelter, or ferretry will back right in, raise their tails, and— bingo! Others, however, delighted with this new sandbox, will soon be digging, rooting, scrabbling, and scattering litter in all directions. Still others, mistaking box for bed, will settle in for a snooze. If your ferret has got the wrong idea about his litter box, it's up to you to set him straight as quickly as possible. Here's how.

Soak up some of his urine on a tissue, put it into the box, and cover it with a thin layer of litter. Add some feces to the back corner. Then, pop in your furball. Sniff, sniff, snuff, snuff—he should quickly get the message that this is his personal toilet facility. But if he's a little slow to catch on, here's another helpful suggestion. Take advantage of the fact that ferrets almost always relieve themselves within minutes of waking up. Pick up your pet right after his snooze, when he starts the telltale backup, and whisk him into the litter pan. He should perform pronto. And you should reward him pronto—perhaps with a lick or two of Ferretone—to reinforce this good behavior. If, however, your pet persists in jumping out of the box without performing, you'll have to be just as persistent and keep popping him back into the box, or even holding him there gently, until you win. Stick to this routine, and before long, most ferrets will be paying regular visits to the box.

But what if your furball steadfastly refuses to go in the corner you've chosen and insists on going in the

Cage clips keep the pan anchored in place.

corner of his choice where there isn't any box? Answer—move the box to where he wants it. It's much easier to change the position of the pan than to change a ferret's mind.

Do you have a stubborn ferret that doesn't seem ready, willing, or able to cooperate in cage training? Then a more radical approach may be called for. Partition off part of the cage, leaving your ferret only enough room for bedding, litter box, and food bowls. Few ferrets fancy soiled food or bedding, so there's no place left for potty but the pan. As soon as visits to the pan become a habit, take down the partition, and restore the romp room.

House Training

Cage training is the easy part of litter training, but you can't keep your ferret in a cage all the time. He needs lots of exercise time outside the cage, so you'll have to get busy on house training right from day one.

And house training is more of a hassle than cage training. Why? When your ferret starts exploring, he's not likely to go looking for a litter box—there are more interesting things to check out. Nor will he trot back into his cage to do his business—he won't want to take a chance on the cage door closing behind him.

So how should you go about house training? The best advice is to start small, one room at a time. If your ferret is going to have only one playroom in the house, obviously this is the place to pick. Otherwise, choose a room that's easily ferret proofed and can be closed off or blocked off from the rest of the house. Put a litter box into any corner you consider convenient—out of the line of traffic and easy to get at for cleaning. Prime it with pee and poop for that lived-in look. Then dab a few drops of Ferretone along the

A ferret that's busy playing won't go too far to look for a litter box.

top edge of the litter box—a little bribery never hurts.

Now wait until your ferret wakes up from a snooze, cuddle him a bit until he starts wiggling, then bring him to the playroom and park him in that pan. If all goes according to plan, he'll go potty right away. This is all the more likely because he has those dabs of Ferretone on the box rim to keep his interest. But ferrets are capricious creatures. Chances are he'll jump out of the box and start exploring. In that case, let him snoop about a bit, but stay a half step behind him and watch for that backward wiggle. Then whisk him right back into the box again . . . and again and again . . . as often as necessary until he delivers the goods.

Success! Dole out lavish praise and a generous reward, hopefully *before* he leaves the box if possible. You want him to make the connection that going in the box equals a goodie. Some ferrets are really quick to catch on to this trick. If your pet's at the top of the ferret IQ scale, he might start popping into that pan for a pretend poop just to get a treat. Don't fall for this ploy—reward performance only.

When confined to a single room, most ferrets will soon be making regular hits in the box. But what if you have a contrary ferret that boycotts the box altogether and insists on making deposits in another corner? Avoid a standoff. When your stubborn ferret won't back down, move the box to where he wants to back up.

Hey, Dad—I'm in the box! Where's my treat?

Training in only one room isn't so bad, it's when you give your pet more rooms to roam that the trouble usually starts. First of all, from a ferret's point of view, every room has more than four corners. See where that end table fits against the wall— a corner! See where that sofa meets the wall—two more corners! And check out the bookcase, the TV stand, the desk—corners, corners, corners! Secondly, timing is important—a ferret's gotta go when a ferret's gotta go. If there's no box nearby, he'll commandeer the nearest corner. Thirdly, consider ferret curiosity. A busybody snooping around the living room when nature calls is highly unlikely to make a dash for that box in the family room.

You could always follow your ferret around morning, noon, and night. But that's not too practical! A better solution is to provide multiple boxes. The fact is, if you allow your ferret to roam the house, he'll need a litter box in every room and two in large rooms. Over time, you'll figure out where your ferret wants them. In spots where a box isn't practical (behind the bed, near a door), put down a piece of plastic carpet runner and cover it with newspaper. The newspaper can be replaced frequently, and the runner protects the flooring underneath.

OOPS! Another Accident

With ferrets, litter box misses are a fact of life. No matter how well you've trained your furball, you'll have to be prepared for the odd little pile of poop behind the sofa or even right next to the litter box. If you're lucky enough to catch your pet in the act, call out "No!", clap your hands loudly, and quickly cart the offender off to the nearest box. Never spank him or rub his nose in the mess. Punishment does more harm than good; it's rewarding good behavior that gets results.

When you find a poop pile but there's no ferret in sight, don't bother to hunt the culprit down and drag him back to the scene of the accident. Ranting and raving after the fact won't register with him. Better just keep your cool and clean up. A tissue is handy for picking up feces. Urine can be soaked up with a paper towel and the wet spot treated with a pet urine neutralizer or a mixture of vinegar and water.

What can be done if your ferret keeps leaving his calling card behind the grandfather clock, underneath the bed, or next to the umbrella stand? Will spray repellents made for dogs and cats repel ferrets, too? In a word, no. So don't waste your money. Instead, try sprinkling some dry ferret food over the area—most ferrets won't mess in their food. Of course, a few smarty pants will simply chow down the grub and then back up. In this case, better buy another box or put down some newspaper.

On occasion, your well-trained ferret might suffer a relapse and take to ignoring his boxes. Don't get too alarmed. He's probably just got a bone to pick with you. Maybe you've been away from home too much recently, working late hours and cutting back on playtime. Maybe there's a new addition to the family—animal or human. Maybe company has upset his routine. Missing the box could be your ferret's way of getting even. A little extra TLC and a large dollop of attention will usually set things straight.

If nothing's new on the home front, your pet might be peeved because the litter pan is too dirty— or even too clean. Some ferrets won't set foot in a used box, and others will turn up their noses at a clean one. Is your ferret a neat freak or a bit of a slob? Only time will tell.

Litter box habits gone haywire can sometimes indicate a medical problem. If you notice dribbling, diarrhea, abnormal stools, or unusually frequent visits to the box, see the vet without delay.

Sorry, Mom—I missed the box.

If All Else Fails

OK, you've given litter training your best shot and that little dunderhead has still not caught on. Don't despair . . . there is a solution. It will just require a bit more effort on your part. Instead of training your ferret to use the box, you'll have to train yourself to monitor his comings and goings so that he doesn't have any opportunity for accidents.

Remember, ferrets usually hit the box soon after waking up, so don't let your ferret out of his cage until he goes potty. When he's out and about, keep an eye on him. Any corner sniffing, any backward wiggling, any tail raising and you'd better scoot him to a box pronto. It's also a good idea to return him to the cage at regular intervals for bathroom breaks. And every time you find him napping around the house, stick him back into the cage so that the litter pan is right under his nose when he wakes up.

Keep it Clean

As a ferret owner, you'll have to resign yourself to poop patrol—or delegate the job to someone else. Daily scooping should be part of your routine. You'll also have to empty each box, clean it out, and renew the contents on a regular basis. How often? This depends on the type of litter you're using. For example, clumping litters won't have to be completely renewed nearly as often as the pelleted types. Between box changes, a wet paper towel comes in handy for wiping out soiled corners. When you do dump the box, wash it out with either an odor-control product like Critter Fresh or Odor-Be-Gone or with a mild bleach/water solution.

It's not just the box you have to keep clean, the flooring around the box needs attention, too. Why? Ferrets scatter litter as they hop in and out of the pan. They also have the annoying habit of dragging their bottoms on the floor just outside the box. Do you really want your carpet

A towel spread under the litter box keeps the floor clean.

used as toilet paper? Here's how to take care of both the tracking and the brown streaks: place an old towel or a newspaper under the box. Don't be stingy with the floor cover—it has to be quite a bit bigger than the box to take care of any mess.

Wrap Up

So now *you* know the ins and outs of litter training. But remember, it may take a little time for your ferret to get the hang of things. Persistence is the name of the game; kindness and patience are the most important ingredients for success. So hang loose and hang in—working as a team, you'll beat those litter box blues.

Chapter Eight

Training

Training Tips

I f you've got a vision of your ferret heeling, sitting, and staying put on command, jumping through hoops, or fetching the newspaper . . . forget it. For these tricks, you need a barking furball. But don't give up on your fuzzy—she has her own unique talents and abilities. It's just a matter of knowing what she's capable of and then training her to do it.

In this chapter, you'll find out what your ferret *can* learn. But before you launch into training, there are some basic training tips for you to keep in mind. The first, and most important, is that 99.9 percent of ferrets don't respond to praise as compensation for their labors. It's not a "Well done!" or a "Way to go!" that will persuade your pet to perform— it's a food reward. Ferrets like their just desserts.

And not just any old food reward will do. Skip the normal supper fare—your ferret won't turn cartwheels for that. Only mouth-watering, lip-smacking, to-die-for treats will do. For a list of tasty treats with real ferret appeal, go back and check the section, "Good Treats," in

Chapter 4. Then, have your ferret do a little taste testing to see which goodie she goes crazy over; this is the treat you need to use for training.

And here's another tip to make training go more smoothly. Keep the training sessions short—ferrets have a short attention span. Although repetition is the name of the game when you're teaching your ferret a new behavior, don't overdo it. Repetition is good; overkill is not. So scrap the marathon training sessions; stick to short, frequent sessions instead.

It's also a good idea to let your frantic fuzzy run around and burn off some of her pent-up energy before training sessions begin. A ferret bounding out of the cage for playtime isn't going to be interested in schooltime right away. So let her run, run, run and explore, explore, explore until she's settled down a bit and can focus on her lessons.

Coming When Called

One of the most important things you can teach your ferret is to come to you when you call her. Or rather, when you squeak for her. For some reason, almost all ferrets will snap to attention when they hear a squeaky toy. Why? Is it because the squeak sounds like mom calling to her kits? Does it sound like a sibling from nest days? None of the ferret experts seem to know why, but most agree on the results. Regardless of why it works, all you need to know is that it does work.

So run on down to your local pet store or discount store and check out the squeaky toys. Choose with great care—not all squeaky toys are ferret friendly. Steer clear of anything made of rubber, latex, and foam. Remember, these materials can be hazardous to your pet if swallowed. What kind of toy *is* safe to bring home? A well-made stuffed toy with a loud, high-pitched squeaker is best. Just make sure it has no eyes, nose, ears, baubles, or anything else that can be chewed off, torn off, or ripped off. And check to see that the squeaker itself is buried deep inside the toy so that it can't be got at.

Although a squeaky toy is the best pet pager, some ferrets come running when they hear other sounds, too. The high pitch of a harmonica or the shake of a box of Cheerios might be music to your ferret's ears. Whatever signal you settle on, stick with it, because switching sounds can confuse your ferret.

OK, you've picked out the treat and the squeaky toy, now it's just a matter of teaching your ferret how to answer the squeak. With some fer-

No treat—no trick!

rets, it's a no-brainer . . . no teaching's necessary. Just squeak, and ten seconds later, you'll be knocked over in the rush. Others don't catch on quite so quickly—they'll need a few lessons. Here's what to do.

Hold a treat a few inches (or centimeters) from your ferret's nose. Squeeze that ol' squeaky toy, and immediately give her the treat. And repeat, repeat, repeat. This teaches your pet to associate the squeak with the treat. Next, hold that goodie a little farther from your furball and *squeak*-treat, *squeak*-treat, *squeak*-treat. Then, it's just a matter of expanding the distance a little bit at a time over several training sessions. Before long, your fuzzy will be coming to you from anywhere in the room or even from the next room. Keep practicing—your goal is to have your fuzzy come running from anywhere in the house when you squeak. And remember, always give her a treat as soon as she answers the squeak.

Coming to a squeaky toy is not just a cute trick. It can be a lifesaver if your ferret gets lost. Do you think she's lost inside? Then squeak around the house and listen. If she's stuck somewhere, you'll likely hear her scratching and scrabbling, trying to get free. Do you think she's lost outside? Then grab the squeaky toy and see "Lost and Found" in Chapter 6.

Of course, your ferret might not be lost, just hiding or snoozing. Again, a squeaky toy will usually bring her running. This is particularly useful when you're already late for school and you need to cage that ferret fast. Be careful, though, that you don't squeak only when you want to cage your critter. If you do, your ferret will soon catch on to the fact that *squeak* doesn't just equal treat—it equals treat and then confinement. It won't take her long to boycott the squeak. After all, what self-respecting, fun-loving ferret's

Squeak-treat.

going to answer a sound that signals the end of playtime?

Sitting Up

Sitting up is a cute trick your ferret can learn—not particularly useful, but really cute. And, it's as easy to learn as it is to teach. Just grab that goodie, hold it in front of your ferret's nose, slowly raise the treat up, and watch your ferret follow it. As soon as she gets to a sitting position, give her the goodie. Then, when she's finished smacking her lips, do it again. She won't take long to master this trick.

However, don't expect her to perform on command. You can't call out "Sit up!" and count on your trainee to obey the order. It's the food, not the command, that persuades your ferret to spring into action.

Shoulder Riding

Some ferrets are partial to shoulder riding. They like a panoramic view of their surroundings. Others like to have their feet firmly planted on the ground—no amount of bribing will persuade them to shoulder sit. You won't know if your pet is fond of heights or afraid of heights until you give it a try.

Start this training by getting down to ferret level. Sit on the floor, and place your pet securely onto your shoulder. Hold her there gently, stroke her, rub her head, whisper sweet nothings in her ear. Dole out a few treats, too. In short, make that shoulder a pretty nice place to be. Let her get the hang of her new perch, but don't overdo things. When she's had enough, let her down. Then try again later.

After a few floor-sitting sessions, if your pet has an easygoing shoulder-sitting attitude, you can graduate from the floor to the edge of a chair. Why a chair, and why the edge of it? When you're sitting on a chair, you're midway between sitting on the floor and standing up. Your ferret gets used to being higher up but still has a safety net in case of bailouts. You sit on the edge of the chair rather than leaning back so that your student can't jump onto the chair back so easily. Slip her the odd treat, and she won't be so interested in slipping off your shoulder.

The next step in training is for you to stand up and walk around with your trainee on your shoulder. Again, bribery works wonders in keeping your ferret planted on your shoulder instead of taking a dive without a parachute. Rides shouldn't be too long. Whenever she's getting fidgety and you sense she's ready to split, let her down before she leaps down.

For those ferrets that have a head for heights, shoulder riding is a great way to bond with their owners. But if your ferret cringes at the mere thought of heights, don't push the shoulder riding. Instead, pop her into a carry bag and let her bond at hip level.

Chapter Nine

Behavior Management

Management versus Training

D ogs, cats, birds, hamsters—all pets have some annoying traits that drive their owners up the wall. Ferrets are no exception. It would be wonderful if you could train them out of their troublesome traits. But, the fact of the matter is that this is not always possible. For example, if your little delinquent can get at your houseplants, no amount of training will discourage him from digging in the dirt. Some behaviors are instinctive and can't be changed. So management rather than training is what you aim for. In other words, go for damage control, not ferret control.

The following sections outline some ideas for dealing with common ferret behaviors that could make your blood pressure rise. In each case, several management options are given because ferrets are individuals—what works for one won't always work for another.

As you're reading through the suggestions, keep in mind that physical punishment is never an option. Never, ever spank your fur-

ball for behaviors that get your goat. He's just doing what comes naturally, so you'd be punishing him for what he can't help. And, anyway, as a responsible pet owner, you should *always* treat your ferret with loving kindness, *never* with physical force.

Caching Compulsion

Caching means hiding stuff. And your wily weasel is an expert at it. Caching is a carryover from predator days. Just what type of stuff will your hoarder hoard? Food is a favorite. Watch your little sneak thief at his food dish—he'll often do a grab and run, making off with a single piece or even a sizable mouthful of dry food. Up to the bedroom he'll scurry, to deposit his goodies into his food bank in the corner. If he's lucky enough to get a meal of canned food for supper, watch out—that might get stashed, too.

All different types of foods are subject to the stash n' cache routine. Dry food isn't a major problem; just pick up the piles on a regular basis. Don't be surprised, though, if your furry friend replaces them as soon as your back's turned. In fact, you can count on it. With canned food, table food, or treats, you have to be more careful about cleanup. Anything that can spoil or mold needs to be picked up pronto.

Caching is one of those behaviors that you can't change. And it doesn't stop at food. Any little objects (or big ones for that matter) that take your ferret's fancy are likely to be heisted and hidden. Watches, keys, remote controls, pop can coolers, pliers with soft grips, wrapped granola bars, favorite toys (yours and his), beepers, socks, and cell phones are all prime targets for the light-fingered looter. Keep in mind that your ferret could have several caches. If you're missing something and it's not in one of your pet's usual hidey holes, then maybe he has a secret stash you haven't ferreted out yet.

And just where is he likely to stockpile his treasures? Try looking behind the grandfather clock, under the sofa or chairs, inside bed box springs, in non-ferret-proofed cupboards or drawers, and in hard-to-reach corners. The more difficult it is for you to get at a spot, the better your ferret will like it. It's important to do the rounds of the various hoards on a regular basis to ensure that your industrious stockpiler hasn't hidden anything that could be hazardous to his health, especially those three ferret favorites—rubber, foam, and sponge.

Remember, you can't stop your ferret from caching. It's up to you to monitor his collections and remove anything that's unsafe.

Carpet Clawing

When your ferret's on one side of a closed door and he hears the family living it up on the other side of the door, guess what side he wants to be on? Since he can't reach the handle to open the door and join you, the only solution he can come up with is to dig his way under the door to get to you—and dig he will till your carpet's in shreds.

What if your ferret has been enjoying that cozy home away from home under the sofa and you block off his access? Again, he'll try to claw his way in. Even months after access has been denied, he'll still be trying to claw his way in, because your ferret is like an elephant—he never forgets.

Unfortunately, carpet clawing is another annoying behavior that you can't train your ferret out of. So, once more, it's up to you to manage the situation and go for damage control. Don't waste your money on sprays made to stop cats and dogs from scratching—they don't deter most ferrets.

An easy solution that works for many ferrets is to cover the attack zone with a piece of clear plastic carpet runner, taped down securely on all sides with wide masking tape or clear packing tape. The tape is important—without it, your digger will dive under the plastic and continue scratching and scrabbling.

Look what I found!

It would be nice if the plastic carpet runner solution would work for all ferrets. But, the truth is, some are not only carpet scratchers, they're tape tearers, too. However, it doesn't cost much to give the idea a try. It might work just fine for your ferret.

If plastic and tape don't foil your fuzzy, here's another idea that might curtail clawing at a doorway. Cut a piece of foot-wide (30 cm wide) Plexiglas or Lucite so that it fits the door opening exactly. Lay it flat on the floor to cover the carpet and keep it in place with a heavy decorative doorstop. This should discourage all but the most diligent diggers. But if your ferret's a really committed carpet clawer that starts clawing the carpet at the sides of the Plexiglas, you may have to cut and notch a larger piece of Plexiglas so that it extends a foot (30 cm) or so beyond the doorway on either side.

So much for doorways—but what about other spots that can be the target of your ferret's destructive attention? When he wants to get under the sofa or under a chair, he'll scratch, scratch, claw, claw. Again, try protecting the carpet with a plastic runner or Plexiglas. This is not an ideal solution in high-traffic areas, but it's better than ripping up the carpet and going to hardwood. (Hey, maybe that's not a bad idea!)

Scrrratch

In his efforts to see life on the other side of the door, a ferret will resort not only to carpet clawing but to door scratching as well. This is another ferret faux pas that doesn't respond to training. So, unless you're partial to distress marks on your door, you'll have to take action to protect the paint work.

A cheap solution is to tape clear-plastic carpet runner to the door with clear packing tape. You won't have to cover the whole door—just the attack zone. However, if your ferret's a tape-tearing terror, forget this idea. He'll be down to the wood in no time.

Another option is to buy a Scat Mat or Pet Mat to place in front of the door. These mats are recognized by humane societies and veterinarians as effective training tools that are particularly useful when nothing else works. They plug into an electric outlet and, when stepped on, produce a tingling sensation like a mild static shock. The mats won't hurt your ferret, but he'll certainly think twice about stepping onto one.

Place the mat directly in front of the door and plug it in. Then when your ferret heads for the door, he'll have to step on the mat. Uh, oh—bad idea! Watch him hightail it in the opposite direction. He might give it another try later, but it won't take long for him to realize he's in a no-win situation. Of course, if you have a little Einstein, he might figure out how to beat the mat. How's he going to do that, you might wonder? Well, if he can't go over it, he'll just wriggle right under it. So if you've got one smart cookie on your hands, it's tape time again! Even tape rippers will often be deterred because it's not easy to get the tape off without touching the mat. Before you use a Pet Mat, read the directions

carefully. Also remove the rubber feet from the power pack—you don't want it to be a snack pack.

One surefire way to prevent your ferret from scratching at the door is to open the door. Of course, he'll bolt right out unless you block off his escape with a substitute door. Both a Weezl Watchr ferret gate or a homemade Plexiglas ferret gate will work. For the complete scoop on these options, see "Setting Boundaries" in Chapter 6.

Did your ferret get to the door before you did? Are there telltale scratches that give him away? Don't worry. A dab of paint, wood stain, or scratch cover will quickly hide the evidence.

Protect Your Houseplants

One thing you can be sure of . . . if you have a houseplant within ferret reach, you'll have a delighted digger diving right in. You'll also have earth *everywhere*—especially if you've just watered the plants and the irresistible smell of damp earth is in the air. Digging and delving in dirt is what ferrets are born to do. You'll never change this instinctive behavior, so you'd better resign yourself to houseplant management—either move those houseplants right out of ferret reach, or else ferret proof the plant pots.

Unless you relocate your plants to a ferret-free room, moving them out

Ferret proof your houseplants by covering the soil with wire mesh and stones.

of ferret reach isn't as simple as it sounds. Do you think those plants that were sitting on the end table are going to be safe up on the kitchen table? Think again! Watch your wily weasel sitting around, sizing up possible ways of getting up onto the table . . . or of dragging the plant down off the table. He'll see the chair, for example, as a ladder to get up or the tablecloth as a conveyor belt to bring the plant down. So it's up to you to make absolutely certain that there's no ferret path to the plants.

If there aren't enough elevated plant perches in your house, or if it's not possible to balance your giant jade on your mini mantel, then your only other course of action is to fer-

ret proof the plant pots. Buy some 0.5-inch (1.3-cm) square galvanized screening, cut it to fit with wire cutters, then place it around the plant on top of the dirt. Now, pile up large landscaping stones or flat river rocks on top of the screening. Water will still be able to trickle through to the plant, but only a hefty Hercules will be able to move the rocks.

It's too bad that this solution won't work for pint-sized plant pots—even with rocks in them, they're easily knocked over. Are there any solutions? You could move the plants. You could also try wall-mounted shelves, hanging planters, or tall free-standing plant stands for those small pots.

Chapter Ten

Ferret Friends

Is an Only Ferret a Lonely Ferret?

One ferret, two ferrets, three ferrets, four—five ferrets, six ferrets, seven ferrets, more? Just what size is your ferret family going to be? Sometimes there isn't much choice. Has Mom insisted on a one-ferret restriction? Does your apartment lease specify one pet only? Is the purchase price of one ferret and the cost of its upkeep as much as your budget can stand? If so, yours will obviously be a one-ferret family. The question is then: Will an only ferret be a lonely ferret?

Don't lose sleep over this concern. An only ferret can manage just fine as long as you lavish him with love and attention. He'll also need plenty of out-of-the-cage playtime and loads of toys to keep him busy. A single ferret will look to his human family for companionship. Don't let him look in vain. Ferrets that are ignored and cage bound suffer from depression and exhibit behavior problems.

However, you don't have to feel guilty if you're out during the day.

Ferrets sleep 14 to 18 hours a day anyway, and your furball will learn to adjust his sleep schedule so that he gets some shut-eye while you're gone and is raring to go when you get back. Just make sure that you're ready to play when he is, because if you can't make time for your pet, maybe it's a tank of fish and not a ferret you should have.

Are Two Right for You?

If you've ever seen two tiny kits rollicking around a pet store cage together, then you know that ferrets enjoy the company of other ferrets. Or, if you've watched the antics of two inseparable adult ferrets, you might get to thinking that two would be right for you. So now the question is are two twice as nice, or are they double trouble? The short answer is two ferret *friends* are twice as nice, but two ferret *foes* are double the trouble.

A pair of bosom buddies will keep each other company when you're out of the house or asleep. Except

Does only mean lonely?

split up . . . they can become grief stricken and depressed if separated.

Two ferret friends are one thing; two ferret foes are quite another. Ferret owners most often run into difficulties when they try to bring home a playmate for an established ferret. If you bring a new Jake home because you think your little Lonny's looking lonesome, there's no guarantee that they'll take to one another. Some ferrets get along just fine when introduced—they hit it off right away. Some go through a period when they fight each other and jockey for dominance—this can go on for hours, days, weeks, or months. And then there are the ones who *never ever* get along, despite your best efforts to foster friendly relations.

Unfortunately, it's impossible to tell in advance how your home buddy will react to a ferret newcomer. There are, however, right ways and wrong ways of going about the getting-to-know-you process. The wrong way is to bring the new guy home and plop him into the home turf cage—chances are the homey ain't gonna like it. Why not? He's used to being head honcho and will want to show the new guy who's boss. And how does a ferret do this? He'll likely hiss, pounce on the newbie, grab him by the neck, shake him, bite him, and drag him around . . . all accompanied by screams from the victim.

If this is the wrong way, what's the right way? To lessen the stress for both pets, it's best to provide a separate cage, bedding, bowls, and

for the initial purchase price and additional veterinary costs, the day-to-day expense for two isn't much more than it is for one—one large cage with furnishings will do for two, a second mouth to feed won't break the bank, and toys can be shared (well most of the time).

The way to be absolutely certain that the critters will be compatible is to pick two littermates or two cage mates that are already best buddies. They're not hard to spot. Just look for the ones that play together, wrestle together, tussle over food, and collapse in a heap to sleep together. Or, go for a pair of adult pals that have always lived together. In fact, two adult ferrets that have been raised together shouldn't be toys for the newcomer. Let him get used to his new environment before there's any question of introductions. The next step is to put the ferret cages close to one another—but not within striking distance—so the ferrets can see each other and become familiar with each other's fragrance. Some ferret owners also find cage swapping helpful. Pop the newcomer into the homeboy's cage while the homeboy goes into the newbie's cage. Again, this is a non-threatening way for the ferrets to get accustomed to each other's scent.

After a few days of long-distance sniffing, cage swapping, and separate playtimes, it's time for a brief face-to-face encounter. Take the ferrets out of their cages, and put them into the play area together with some toys. You'll need to stick around to supervise. What can you expect? If you're lucky, they'll just sniff around each other's neck and anal area, tussle a bit, then start to play. In many cases, the sniffing and tussling will lead to battling and brawling. Don't separate them every time scrapping occurs, or the dominance issue will never be worked out between them. However, battle scars are not allowed!

To help even things up for the underdog, spray his back and neck with Bitter Apple spray or smear those areas with Bitter Apple cream. The aggressor won't be so quick to pounce and grab when he gets a mouthful of bitter fur for his efforts. Keep this first encounter short—ten minutes max.

However, if at any time they really start a major battle, separate them immediately—you don't want one of the ferrets to get hurt. What's the best way to get them apart? Protect yourself with a pair of heavy gloves, squirt the bully with water from a spray bottle, and then return the opponents to their separate cages. After a ding-dong battle, you might not be too anxious to put them together again. But, you have to keep at it if you're going to have any chance of success. Keep using the Bitter Apple, keep up the daily get-togethers, and keep the encounters brief. When you see signs of progress, gradually increase their time together. Be aware that this whole process may take a while. In fact, it could take up to eight months for the ferret foes to become fast friends (or at least to tolerate each other).

Two's company.

Be aware, too, that despite your best efforts, there are some ferrets that will never get along. If one ferret declares all-out war on the other and their encounters always lead to big battles, don't force the issue for months on end. The underdog will get too stressed. Instead, resign yourself to separate cages, separate litter boxes, and separate playtimes for the fighting ferrets.

Please use common sense when fostering togetherness. For example, a kit should never be subjected to an aggressive adult—the kit won't have a chance of coming out on top, and constant combat will be very stressful. So if a kit comes under attack, wait until it's at least six months old before trying introductions again. And forget about male bonding between unaltered males—they're so territorial that fighting is inevitable. For uncastrated males, hyped up on hormones, bachelor apartments are the way to go.

Lemme at him!

Multiferret Families

Is your family crazy about ferrets? Would you be happy to bring a whole litter home? Before jumping in with both feet, ask yourself these important questions.

• Do you have the money it takes for yearly preventative veterinary care and for unforeseen medical expenses? For example, multiple immunizations mean multiple fees—does your vet give group discounts? Or, 1 misplaced Superball $\div$ 5 curious ferrets = 5 intestinal obstructions = 5 vet bills. *You* do the math.

• Do you have enough time on your hands to care for multiple ferrets? It takes a dedicated household to groom, to bathe, to play with, and to keep track of a group of ferrets—not to mention the time spent on poop patrol!

• Do you have the patience it takes to train several ferrets? Ferrets don't come preprogrammed for litter training and leash walking.

• Do you have the extra space for extra cages if personality clashes make habitat sharing impossible?

• Have you checked to make sure that there aren't any local by-laws restricting the number of pets you can have?

If you can answer yes to all of these questions, then by all means, open your heart and open your home to as many rascals as you can realistically manage. You'll have a riot and so will they. But *PLEASE* don't ever take on more ferrets than you can cope with or afford. Each ferret

Are you a ferret fanatic? Is a whole crew right for you?

deserves the best-possible life, and as a responsible owner, it's up to you to see that each one gets it.

Ferrets and Other Pets

So you're a die-hard pet lover? Are you wondering if a ferret will fit into your menagerie? A ferret can be a welcome addition to your animal family as long as some precautions are taken. And, if you already own a ferret and want to add another pet, that's often possible, too.

Cats and dogs are probably the most popular pets. Can ferrets get along with cats? The good news is that most ferrets and most cats can learn to live with each other. Depending on each animal's personality, they'll either become great friends or maybe just tolerate each other. Kits and kittens raised together have the best chance of peaceful cohabitation. However, if you're introducing a kit to a full-grown cat or a kitten to a full-grown ferret, you'll need to proceed with caution—the larger animal could attack the smaller one.

Never attempt any cross-species introductions without adult supervision. Both animals should be held by adults and allowed to sniff and touch noses. Don't let them down onto the floor together until they seem tolerant of one another. Any hissing, swatting, spitting, arching of backs, displaying of teeth, swishing of tails, or bristling of fur is a sign that they're *not* ready to hit it off just yet. Don't give up, though. They probably need more time to get used to each other. Twice daily encounters of the hand-held kind should soon get them over the getting-to-know-you hurdle and onto the floor for more personal contact. With time, most cats and ferrets do establish an easygoing, or at least tolerant, relationship. However, if either cat or ferret shows any signs of going on the attack, keep them separate.

Even greater care is necessary when ferrets and dogs are sharing the same living quarters. It's not at all advisable to have a ferret loose when a terrier-type or hunting dog is in the house, too. These dogs have been bred to attack and kill animals that look very ferretlike. Why take the chance? However, if you have a gentle-natured dog that is not prone to snapping, there's a good chance

Rodents and ferrets don't mix.

that ferret and dog can become good buddies. It's the personality of each animal that counts here. Is your ferret laid back or a little hellion? Will he be unruffled or riled up by an occasional sniff or lick from the dog? Will your dog tolerate a mischievous ferret nipping at his heels or pulling at his ears? Will he put up with ferret raids on his food dish?

Again, when the introductions start, proceed with caution and with adult supervision. And again, if there's *any* concern about compatibility, scrap the matchmaker plans, and keep the animals apart.

There are some house pets that your ferret would love to get to know better . . . but as a headhunter, not as a friend. Your ferret should have *absolutely no access* to *hamsters, gerbils, mice, rats, guinea pigs, rabbits, chinchillas, birds, lizards, fish, frogs, or turtles.* Not that all ferrets would harm all of these pets, but you have to remember that ferrets still have predatory instincts—don't provide them with prey. You may think that Hammy's perfectly safe in his hamster habitat or that Gus the guppy is out of harm's way in his aquarium or that Polly is securely barricaded in her birdhouse, but don't be too sure. Ferrets can open cage doors, lift the lids off fish tanks, and stick their paws through cage wires. So, if you want to keep a ferret in the same house as a rodent, a reptile, a fish, or a feathered friend, the little pets need to be right up out of ferret reach or confined to a room that's strictly off-limits to the ferret.

Chapter Eleven
Fun with Your Ferret

The Fun Never Ends

With ferrets around, the fun is fast and furious. Party, party, party is the motto of kits and adult ferrets alike. Cats may become aloof and sedate with age; the fun-loving ferret goes through life gamboling and frisking like a kitten. And, she won't sit around waiting till you're ready for action—your furball will take the initiative, seeking you out and coaxing you to please play.

That's what the weasel war dance is all about! When she arches her back, puffs up her fur, and leaps around in a frenzy, she's pleading, "Come and get me, I wanna play!" Who can resist? Playtime is fun time—both for you and your ferret. Just as important, playtime keeps your pet physically fit and mentally alert. Remember, she sleeps a lot during the day, so when she's awake, she needs the opportunity to burn off energy and to stimulate the old brain cells. Playtime also teaches your ferret social skills. She uses play to test her limits with the people in her life and to bond with family members.

Interactive Games

Think back to the games you enjoyed as a kid. These are just the sort of games that will appeal to the kid in your ferret. Well, jump rope and hopscotch may be a bit beyond her, but hide-and-seek, tag, and peekaboo will all get the four thumbs up from your furball.

Start with hide-and-seek. Ferrets seem preprogrammed for this game. When you see your ferret ducking out of sight under the furniture, make a big deal about running to find her. Call out "I'm coming to get you!", tap on the floor with your hands, and watch her come scurrying out. Now it's your turn to run and hide. Crouch down behind a chair and yell "Come and get me!" Your pet will come careening around the corner, dooking and dancing happily, eager to find you. This is a good game for family fun—though you'll have to be careful that, in all the excitement, your ferret doesn't get under foot.

You can teach your ferret to play tag in the traditional way where you chase her and she chases you. Get on your hands and knees, closer to

A pull toy makes for a great game of tag.

ferret level, and scramble after her. Then head off in the opposite direction so that she can race after you. (Watch your toes!) She'll get the hang of the game in no time. To get you off your knees, why not try another version of tag? In this variation, your pet chases a toy. A toddler's pull toy on wheels is ideal, or a favorite stuffed toy tied to a shoestring works well, too. This game is a no-brainer. Just run around, hauling the toy behind you, and your furry friend will give chase as fast as her little legs can go. Be fair—let her catch it every so often!

Peekaboo may be a baby's entertainment, but your ferret will also go gaga over this game. In peekaboo, you take advantage of the fact that ferrets like to hide under sofas, chairs, or beds. When you see the little rascal diving under the bed, creep up and tap the dust ruffle. This is the signal for your pet to poke her nose

out at the spot where you're tapping. When you see the nose, sing out "Peekaboo! I see you!" and rub her nose. Then tap at another spot on the ruffle, and your pet will shoot off to begin the game all over again. If you're in the living room or family room where there's several pieces of skirted furniture, it's surprising how long your ferret will keep the game going, dashing from sofa to loveseat to chair, clucking as she goes.

War Games

Ferrets like to roughhouse, and rowdy games are right up their alley. Mock war games give them a chance to indulge in the boisterous horseplay they enjoy. Just watch out, though—if your ferret gets too excited and her behavior too unruly, it's time to call a truce before you or your ferret gets hurt.

Mock combat is a ferret favorite. First, you and your ferret need to take up battle stations on the floor. Next, ball your hand into a loose fist. Then, while darting your hand back and forth on the floor in front of your ferret's nose, tempt her to jump at it. As she pounces, move your hand around some more—keep her guessing. When she scores a direct hit, turn her over and tickle her tummy. These skirmishes can get fast and furious with attack and counterattack, but if the combat ceases to be mock, cease and desist immediately.

What would a war be without bombs? Sock bombs, that is. Roll up a pair of socks into a ball, take aim, and toss the sock bomb toward the ferret target. Arc the bomb in the air so that it lands gently at your foe's feet. She'll promptly pounce on it, sink her teeth into it, and shake the living daylights out of it. (In view of this combative behavior, you might be well advised to construct your bombs out of old, holey socks!) Sock missiles will be a hit with your furry foe—she'll be happy to engage in battle as long as the barrage of bombs keeps coming.

Tug-of-war anybody? Grab an old tube sock and knot it, or an old towel, or an old sweatpant leg, or splurge on a dog tug toy. Wiggle the "rope" in front of your fuzzy's nose. It won't take much tempting for her to grab the end and start pulling. Heave, ho!—she'll yank on her end, tugging and tussling, twisting and turning, with a few hisses and bounces thrown in for good measure. But just remember, it's a ferret on the other end of the rope, not the local fire department. So to avoid any broken ferret teeth, don't get rough with the yanking. Gently does it is the rule for this game.

If you're using a towel as a tug toy, you can also turn it into a ferret troop transporter. Just drag it along the floor, and your ferret foot soldiers will run after it and hop aboard for a ride.

Ball Games

Balls, balls, and more balls . . . give your ferret a few Ping-Pong balls and she'll be in ferret heaven. Roll one across the kitchen floor, then stand back and watch the fun. Your fuzzy will run after it, trap it under her chest with her paws, then scuttle backward. She'll roll over, pop it up in the air, and chase it again. Roll three across the floor and triple the fun.

Ping-Pong balls are ferret favorites.

When she gets tired of the chase, toss a batch of balls into a box. Pop in your pet, and get your camera rolling. You'll want to capture all the action as balls and ferret fly in every which direction.

Make a few Ping-Pong balls part of the cage decor—they'll help your ferret to stay busy when you're too busy to play. Examine the balls from time to time—any cracked ones should be tossed into the trash. Dented ones can be restored to bounceability by plopping them into boiling water. If this trick doesn't pop out the dents, ditch the dented balls—cracked or dented balls can be ripped apart easily by your ferret, and sharp bits of ball are a hazard if swallowed.

Tennis balls are also ferret friendly as long as they're intact. And some cat balls are OK, too. The solid plastic kind with bells or rattles inside are a hit with furballs, but stay away from the kind with holes that could snare a ferret's tooth. Nix golf balls (too hard), wiffle balls (too many holes), and any fancy balls that could have pieces ripped off and swallowed. Never, ever, ever give your pet a rubber, sponge, or foam ball. This means no Nerf balls, no cute little dimpled cat balls, and absolutely no Superballs. Remember, rubber, sponge, and foam can cause intestinal blockage—what starts out as fun could end up being fatal.

One ball that will really get your ferret going is a treat ball. Fill it with tiny treats, and open the trap door. As your ferret rolls it around, what a great surprise! Every so often a treat drops out. "Hey, mom—how'd that happen?"

Toys for Ferrets

Ferrets have got quite a short attention span—think two-year-old toddler. You can't give your ferret a toy and expect it to keep her occupied all afternoon. It just won't happen. Variety is the spice of ferret life, so when it comes to toys, multiple choice is more fun. But it won't be more fun for you if it breaks the bank. Fortunately, you have a choice here; you can take the ritzy route or the pinchpenny path. Your ferret won't know the difference.

On the pet store shelves you'll find ferret balls and boats, each with several openings for easy entrances and exits. Your ferret will have a ball investigating the ins and outs of

Where's the treat?

these molded plastic toys. When she's finished her explorations, she'll enjoy camping out in her own ferret tent if she hasn't already crashed out in the ball. To liven up tent life, throw in a plastic grocery bag "ground sheet" and a few Ping-Pong balls. Or, dangle a ferret chew bone on a string in front of the tent opening— your camper will bat and swat at it or leap and lunge as she tries to grab it.

Then there are fabric ferret tunnels. With one or two of these, your ferret can do what comes naturally—tunnel in, tunnel out, lie down, and take a snooze. You can also roll her around in one. For a real blast, look for one that comes jazzed up with sound effects—racket sacks crinkle and crackle as your pet burrows through.

A cat wand with feathers on the end can entertain your furry friend for minutes, at least. Switch the wand back and forth in front of your bundle of energy, and she'll jump and gyrate trying to grab it. But don't let her nab it, at least not for keeps, or those fancy feathers will be tattered feathers in no time.

Like toddlers, some ferrets are fond of stuffed animals. Either they get a charge out of chasing them— so go on, drag Teddy around the floor. Or, they prefer the grab-and-run routine, carrying Teddy off and caching him in the stash. The stuffed animals that top the list are the ones with arms, legs, necks, and hair made from braided cotton string.

When buying a stuffed animal or borrowing one from the kids'

Hiding out in a ferret tent.

bedroom, make sure it's ferret safe— no button noses, no wiggly eyes, no bows, no pompoms, no visible squeaker parts. In other words, nothing that could be torn off and eaten.

A word of advice—just because something in the pet shop is labeled "for ferrets" doesn't necessarily mean that it's safe for ferrets. For example, there are some ferret-specific rubber toys on the market. Your pet will go crazy over these, but her sharp teeth could easily chew off chunks that she could swallow. Why take a chance with these rubber toys when biodegradable Cheweasels and Super Chew Ferret Toys are safe alternatives?

Does your budget not allow for store-bought toys? Don't worry. With a little imagination, you can turn everyday items into fun ferret toys. Rummage through the closets, and find a pair of old sweatpants or outgrown jeans. Cut off the legs, and give them to your ferret. She'll have tons of fun in these homemade tunnels.

Tickled pink with a cat wand.

When she crawls out of the tunnels, why not take her for a ride in her very own wagon? It's a snap to make one from a large shoe box or a similar-sized cardboard box. Just pierce one end of the box, and thread a shoelace through the hole. All aboard! Ferrets only, please. Your fuzzy will sit back and enjoy the ride as you haul her around the living room. However, be careful to avoid sharp turns—you don't want her flying out.

Here's another box idea. Take a box about 3 or 4 inches (7.5 to 10 cm) high, or cut a taller one down to size. Cut about half-a-dozen holes, 2 inches (5 cm) in diameter, at random

This is my toy.

all over the box. Now, plop it on top of your pet, and *gently* poke and tickle the rascal through the holes. Keep those fingers moving—what makes the game such fun is that she never knows where the darting digits will come from next. Most ferrets love this game, but never play it with a nipper. You don't want to encourage bad habits.

Here's a cheap alternative to ferret balls and boats. Buy a gallon (3.8 liter) milk jug or an extralarge spring water jug (look for the 4 gallon or 11 liter size). Cut out a few holes, 4 inches (10 cm) in diameter, and smooth the edges with fine sandpaper. Let your investigators loose to explore their new toy. They'll probably fight over who's going to sleep in it first! A similar idea is to use a big, clear-plastic pretzel jar. No need to cut any holes—the open mouth makes for easy entry.

Did you know that on every trip to the grocery store, you're bringing home ferret toys? Yes, those plain old plastic grocery bags are a big hit with almost every ferret. To make them ferret friendly, cut off the handles. Then you won't have to worry about stuck heads or choking ferrets. Throw one bag or many onto the floor, and leave your ferrets to it. They'll dive in head first, roll around in the bags, twist and turn, and cluck like crazy. You can join in the fun by dragging them around in a bag and swirling it around on the floor. Or, you could double bag the ferrets and swing them gently from side to side. Don't go overboard on this

one—you don't want any seasick ferrets. The occasional ferret is prone to eating plastic. If you have one that falls into this category, DO NOT let her play with plastic bags. Instead, provide paper bags for her and for the rest of the gang.

Now that your ferrets are equipped with a bag swing, how about a slide to go with it? In the hardware store look for smooth PVC pipe, 4 to 5 inches (10 to 13 cm) in diameter. Buy a section about 5 feet (150 cm) long—any shorter and the slide will be too steep. Position the pipe so that one end is leaning against the sofa cushion and the other end reaches the floor. At first, you might have to show your fuzzies what the slide is all about—put one through it head first. When they catch on, you might have to exercise crowd control up at the top.

To round out the playground, why not add a sandbox? Your ferrets will certainly appreciate it because digging in dirt is your ferrets' idea of ultimate fun. Remember the houseplants? With a sandbox, they can dig to their heart's content—all with your blessing. Sandboxes come in all shapes and sizes. An extralarge dishpan will do. A large, plastic storage box will work as well. Or you could really go to town and make a deluxe model from a large, plastic garbage can. Cut a few holes, 4 inches (10 cm) in diameter, in the side of the can about 6 inches (15 cm) from the bottom. Pour in 2 to 3 inches (5 to 7.5 cm) of playbox sand and potting soil mixed together. You

1 ferret + 1 plastic grocery bag = a good time

won't have to show your ferrets what to do—they'll smell the dirt and come running. You might want to schedule this activity right before bath time because after all that burrowing and tunneling, they'll be pretty grubby. In the wintertime, substitute snow for sand and let the little diggers get going on snow forts.

Tunnel Fun

No ferret playground would be complete without a tunnel setup. Again, you can go the store-bought route or the homemade route. On the pet store shelves look for ferret-specific flexible vinyl or hard-plastic tunnels. Join several together with elbows, T's, and end caps, and add matching ferret balls for a mind-boggling maze. Your imagination is limited only by your pocketbook. These tunnels can be clear or colorful, but all are see-through, allowing you to watch the lively inside action. Ferret tested and approved, they're a good investment because they have long-lasting appeal both for kits and older ferrets alike.

For do-it-yourselfers, the hardware store sells ferret tunnels, a.k.a. plastic corrugated drainage pipe, a.k.a. plastic weeping tile. Make sure you get the 4-inch (10 cm) diameter tubing; a bigger ferret could get stuck in the 3-inch (7.5 cm) size. Draw up a plan; it's up to you to decide on a layout that fits the ferret room. The pipe can be left in long sections or cut into shorter sections. If you're not handy with a hacksaw, have the store cut it for you, then smooth off the rough edges with fine sandpaper. Connect the sections together with T's, Y's, and elbows for a challenging configuration. The one drawback to the drain pipe system is that, once your ferret disappears inside, she's lost to view until she decides to reappear.

You could also buy really long sections of the tubing and drape it up and over footstools, wind it around behind chairs, and lead it up or down short flights of steps. Because it's corrugated, your ferret can get a grip and climb it like steps.

The beauty of both store-bought and homemade tunnels is that you can start out small and add extra sections as the budget allows. Both types can be easily washed with hot, soapy water to get rid of that familiar ferret fragrance—throw them into the laundry tub, the bathtub, or use the hose outside. Rinse them well so there's no soapy residue for your ferret to lick.

Just running the tubes will keep your burrower busy—change the layout from time to time to keep her guessing. And, if you want to get in on the fun, how about a game of ferret fishing? Tie a ferret bone to a shoestring, then dangle it into the vertical mouth of a T joint. Jangle the bone against the side of the tube, and your alert tunneler will scurry to investigate. While lying on her back, she'll swat, bat, bite, and grab at the bait. Haul the bone out and drag it along the top of the corrugated tube to the next opening. Then, dangle again. The resonating noise will lead your ferret to the next fishing hole. Have fun!

Ferret Fairs and Shows

Another way to have fun with your ferret is to participate in ferret fairs or ferret shows. At these events you'll meet like-minded ferret fanciers with whom you can compare notes—you can also pick their brains for advice and handy hints. Shows are also a great place to see a wide variety of different ferrets. And, if you're in the market for a new ferret, you'll probably find more choices than you would locally. Last but not least, you'll have unlimited opportunities to show off your fur-ball. Bragging about your baby is one of the main pleasures of a ferret show!

Ferret shows are very similar to major cat and dog shows. If you want your ferret to compete at sanctioned shows, you'd be well-advised to get precise information about the show venue, the vaccination requirements, and the competition standards well in advance. Different shows adhere to different standards, and judging is done according to specific guidelines. But if your silver mitt has only three white feet instead

Is it an empty pretzel jar? No, it's a ferret barrel of fun.

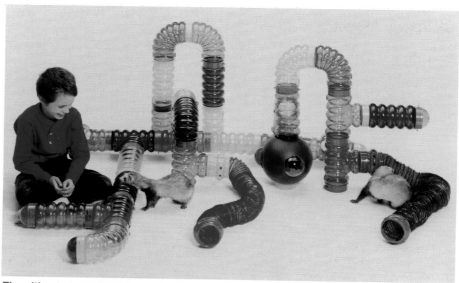

The ultimate tunnel playground.

of four, don't despair. Many shows offer fun categories as well as the championship categories. Your winsome Winnie might not win Best of Show, but she could win Best Behaved or Best Yawner. To get more information about show standards and upcoming events across the country, check the Internet or contact one of the major ferret clubs.

Ferret fairs are generally more relaxed get-togethers—with the emphasis on camaraderie rather than on competition. Why not make a ferret fair a family affair? You can all cheer on the family pet in the paper bag escape contest or in the tube racing. Or, you can put your heads together and devise a great costume for the best-dressed ferret contest.

Whether your ferret's taking a shot at Best of Show or entering the tube races, whether you're there for the competition or just to mix and mingle with other ferret owners, one thing's for sure. Ferret shows and fairs are great fun for family and ferret alike.

Chapter Twelve

Out and About with Your Ferret

Ferrets on the Go

Most ferrets are sociable critters. They like to get out and about, they like to meet people, they like to see the sights. So why not plan on taking your buddy along when you're running around doing errands or visiting friends? Your ferret will enjoy a change of scene, and you'll enjoy the company.

It's best to expose your ferret to new people and new places from as young an age as possible. Why? A kit that's trotted around a lot will soon learn to take new faces and new places in his stride. He'll grow into a friendly, outgoing, and confident adult. Older ferrets that haven't been accustomed to a life on the go can get to like it, but it may take patience and extra effort on your part—don't try too much too soon. If, however, you have a homebody that's not at all happy when he's away from the home turf, don't insist on carting him around—he'll just be miserable. Not every ferret is a gad-about. In fact, some ferrets become distressed, anxious, and frightened when they're away from their own familiar environment. These worrywarts are best left at home.

Here's another point to consider . . . never let strangers pet your ferret. Why? Even a normally gentle ferret might nip at strangers in a strange environment. If the nip is reported, this could lead to problems with local health authorities. In fact, in a worst-case scenario, your pet could be confiscated and put down (see "Immunizations" in Chapter 15). Also, people can transmit a variety of viruses to your ferret. Don't take a chance on your ferret coming down with a cold, the flu, or any other virus . . . keep strangers at arm's length.

Leash Walking

Most ferrets love to get outdoors for a daily walk. Well, maybe *walk* is a bit of a misnomer—a daily sniff and snoop is closer to the truth. However, before you take him outside to pound the pavement, you

Many ferrets enjoy outings with their owners.

need to get your ferret accustomed to a harness and leash inside.

First, take a trip to the pet store to size up the harnesses and leashes. For leash walking, your ferret must have a harness, not a collar, because a ferret can wriggle out of a collar far too easily. There are lots of harnesses on the pet shop shelves, so what kind is suitable for a furball? An H harness is the best bet—they're easy to put on and take off, they're difficult to escape from, they come in a variety of sizes, and, for the fashion-conscious ferret, they come in an array of wild colors. You should find a good selection in both the ferret section and the kitten section of the store. Another possibility is a figure-eight kitten harness. This type isn't quite so easy to put on or to adjust unless you have a pretty placid pet, but it is fairly escape proof when

properly fitted. A third type is a ferret-specific harness/leash that combines a leather body harness with a cord and toggle.

Whichever kind you choose, it's the fit that counts—not so loose that your ferret can escape but not so tight that it's uncomfortable. The rule of thumb is that you should just be able to squeeze the tip of your pinkie under the harness.

Most ferret harnesses come with a matching leash. If you've chosen a kitten harness, you'll probably have to buy a leash separately. Anything lightweight, 3 to 4 feet (90 to 120 cm) long, will do. A swivel hook on the end will help prevent twists and tangles when walking. Do you have two ferrets to walk? A lightweight coupler attached to the end of the leash allows you to walk both of them together, side by side.

Now it's time for some indoor practice to get your ferret used to the harness and leash and to make sure you have the harness fit correctly so that he can't escape. For best results, don't try this until you and your ferret have bonded. The first step is to harness up your ferret. Some fuzzies comply without a fuss. Others fight the fitting tooth and nail. Do you have a bucking bronco on your hands? If so, it's a good idea to use a harness with Velcro fastenings. This type is quicker and easier to put onto a fighting ferret.

When your ferret's buckled up, let him run around his play area to get used to the feel of his gear. No leash yet, please. Some ferrets will go about their business as usual, completely oblivious to the harness. Others will fret and fight, rolling around on the ground, trying to ditch the new equipment. Is your pet a harness hater? Don't force the issue.

A coupler will let you walk two furballs at once.

Don't insist that he wear it for hours on end. Get him used to the offending equipment gradually. Five minutes a day is good for starters, then increase the wearing time bit by bit until he's desensitized to the harness. Only then is it time to attach the leash and get in some *indoor* walking practice.

Guide your ferret gently with the leash. Never yank him, jerk him, tug him, or haul him off his feet. The idea here is not for you to walk *him* around but for him to lead *you* around. As soon as your ferret feels comfortable on the leash, it's time to dispense with the indoor practice

An H harness with matching leash.

Wood . . .

. . . brick . . .

. . . concrete. Get your fuzzy used to walking on different surfaces.

out the orders "Heel," "Sit," or "Stay"—they'll go right over your fuzzy's head. He's just not programmed to understand them. So forget the regimented, owner-in-control walk—to a ferret, a walk is a wander. However, with repeated practice, many ferrets learn to stay to the left or the right of their owner's feet. Encourage this so that your pet's less likely to crisscross in front of you and trip you up or be trodden on. But don't expect that your obedience training will go much further than this. Again, gentle guiding is the way to go.

Do you have an uncooperative walker, one that scoots backward instead of heading forward, or a reluctant one that stubbornly refuses to move? Try this technique that exploits your ferret's natural instincts. Set him down where buildings and sidewalk meet, or where grass and sidewalk meet, or, if you live on a quiet street, where curb and street meet. Ferrets have a tendency to follow along a raised boundary.

When you're out on your walks together, there are a few things that

and head for the great outdoors. (Your ferret does have his distemper shots, doesn't he?)

Right at the outset you have to realize that the four-footed friend on the end of your leash is a ferret, not a dog. So there's no point in barking you have to be on guard against. For example, dogs on the loose are a real hazard where ferrets are concerned. They can appear out of nowhere and pounce on your pet if you're not keeping your eyes open. Any time an unleashed dog appears on the horizon, don't wait to see if it's ferret friendly. Treat any stray dog as a potential threat; scoop your ferret off the ground and scurry out of sight. In fact, it's a good idea to scoop your ferret up even if you meet a leashed dog. Why take any chances? You have no guarantee that the dog's owner has complete control of his or her canine.

Noise is another potential problem. Your ears are accustomed to street noise, but are your ferret's? If your pet's a reluctant walker, it may be because he's afraid of honking horns, backfiring cars, rumbling trucks, wind in the trees, stomping feet, or any number of unfamiliar sounds. Some ferrets are more skittish than others when it comes to noise. So, the strategy here is to start with very short walks every day, and, if your ferret shows any phonophobia (fear of noise), pick him up and reassure him. Carry him home if necessary, and try again tomorrow. Most ferrets will become desensitized to the noises by repeated exposure to them; others will always be fearful. If yours is a sound-sensitive soul, it's kinder to forget the outdoor walks and restrict exercise to the indoors.

There are also environmental hazards to consider when you're out and about with your speed walker. In the summer, watch out for grass that has recently been sprayed or fertilized. In the winter, watch for sidewalks that have been salted. Herbicides and pesticides can poison your pet, and sidewalk salt can burn delicate footpads. Never take your pet outside when the temperature's too hot or too cold. Ferrets are prone to heatstroke—keep them home when it's hot. And although ferrets can tolerate cold much better than heat, don't be fooled by their fur coats. A ferret that's raised indoors doesn't develop a thick-enough coat to withstand freezing temperatures for long.

No matter where you're planning to walk your pet—on the concrete sidewalk, on the grass in your backyard, on the gravel paths at your local park—try to expose him to a variety of walking surfaces so he won't balk at unfamiliar ground. However, in the summer, be wary of pavement that's too hot for ferret feet. Also keep your eyes peeled for foreign objects that could tempt your ferret's weird taste buds. He won't turn up his nose at a litterbug's trash—it's up to you to steer him clear of any debris that could be detrimental to his health such as cigarette butts, foam cups, wads of gum, animal feces, or discarded food. It's also up to you to make sure he doesn't add to the debris by leaving his own little calling cards. No matter where or when your ferret's walking, always carry a pooper scooper. And, use it!

Pet In a Pouch

Sometimes it's more convenient to carry your pet around in a carry bag than to walk him on a leash. When you're in a hurry, when you're in a crowd, when the weather's not too good—these are the times your pet will prefer to be a pouch potato.

There are all sorts of carry bags that will serve the purpose. First, check out the made-for-ferret bags at the pet stores, in mail-order catalogs, or on the Internet. You're spoiled for choice. These bags run the gamut from basic to designer. They come in a wide range of patterns and color. Many are fleece lined. Some double as sleep sacks. It's a good idea to look for one that comes complete with an interior hook—latching your buddy's harness to the hook will prevent unexpected bailouts.

If you're handy with a sewing machine, it's a breeze to run up a homemade bag. Basically, all you need is a piece of heavy-duty material (fleece backed is nice and cozy) about 15 inches (40 cm) wide × 30 inches (75 cm) long. Fold it over so that you get a square 15 inches (40 cm) × 15 inches (40 cm), sew up the side seams, and stitch a narrow hem at the top to prevent fraying. Then, take a piece of polypropylene tape, 45 inches (115 cm) long and 1.5 inches (3.8 cm) wide, and attach each end securely to the bag to form a carrying strap. Keep your ferret safe in this custom-made carrier by securing a swivel hook to a piece of polypropylene tape 0.5 inches (1.3 cm) wide and then stitching the tape inside the bag.

Is sewing not your cup of tea? Don't worry. You may already have a bag around the house that can be pressed into service as a pet carry bag. What about that baby diaper bag that's waiting around for your next garage sale? Or what about your teenager's backpack that's in perfect shape but out of fashion? Do you have a baby snuggle sack around? Just sew up the legs and you're all set. Small gym bags, carry-on bags, or overnight bags are fine as long as they have good ventilation. Ditto with large shoulder bags and purses. A word of caution here, though . . . before popping your ferret into any of these, check the insides thoroughly for any foam, rubber, or sponge. Check, too, for any potentially dangerous doodads that could be bitten off, gnawed off, or chewed off.

When you've found the perfect pouch, don't just drop your ferret in and take off for the day. Not all ferrets are born pouch loungers. Start by letting your pet get used to the bag in the house. Put it onto the floor in his play area, and let him investigate it. When he's used to it, plop him into the pouch and carry him around the house for short periods. Slipping him a treat or two will help him to enjoy the ride. Over a period of a few days, increase his time in the carry bag. Before long, he'll be a seasoned pro.

If, however, you have a rambunctious renegade who keeps trying to fly the coop, here are some ideas for keeping him in the bag. Put him in after playtime when he's all tuckered out—if you're lucky, he'll be too tired to play truant. Whenever he tries to bail, hold him gently but firmly inside the bag, pet him, speak to him, and increase his treat allotment. It's important not to let him out whenever he struggles to escape. He has to learn that he's not the boss; you are. However, if your ferret keeps wiggling and struggling, he could need a bathroom break. Scoot him to the litter box and then back to the bag again.

If, after your best efforts, it's apparent that your pet's not pouch happy, don't push it. Some ferrets will never be cooperative passengers. Do you have a ferret that refuses to ride? Then cut your losses—turn that cozy carry bag into a comfy sleep sack.

When planning a carry bag outing, be sure to take along food and water, harness and leash, and plastic baggies for poop scooping. Keep a close eye on the weather, and head for home if the temperature turns unfit for man or beast. Remember, heat is particularly dangerous for your furball.

Public Transit

Pets are not always welcome on public transit. If you have any plans for boarding bus, subway, streetcar, or train with your furry friend in tow, you'd better call in advance and

Peeping out from a pouch.

check out the company's pet policy. Even if the company gives you an OK, is it a wise move to ferry your fuzzy around on the public system? Busses and subways are busy and noisy—they could be overwhelming for your pet. And, how can you be sure that the temperature at the station or in the vehicle is fit for your ferret? You can't.

So for your ferret's sake, you'd be better off to scrape up the extra cash and take a taxi. But be sure to find out first if pet passengers are accepted. In some major cities, pet taxis are available, but in most towns and cities you'll have to opt for a people taxi. You might stand a better chance of a ride if your ferret's

Never smuggle your pet onto public transit.

in a pet carrier. Another option is to call a friend with wheels (preferably not bicycle wheels) and negotiate for a lift.

Car Travel

When it's a question of getting from point A to point B, a car is definitely the preferred mode of ferret transportation. There are, however, rules for the road. First and foremost, don't let that furball run free; keep him confined at all times. Don't forget, ferrets are the original snoops. You don't want them sniffing out electric wires, rubber hoses, foam stuffing, ashtray goodies, kid's clutter, or yesterday's lunch. Running around in the car could not only jeopardize your pet's safety, it could jeopardize yours, too. A loose ferret is an accident waiting to happen— can you really concentrate on driving

when the little live wire is weaving around your feet, hopping on your shoulder, or crawling over your lap? Of course not! So for safety's sake, when your ferret's traveling in a car, he should be in a cage, a travel carrier, or hooked to a seat belt.

It's easy to hook your pet up to a seat belt. First, do up the passenger seat belt. Next, put your ferret into his harness and attach the leash. Now, wrap and tie the leash around the latched seat belt, giving him just enough length to move comfortably but not enough leeway to jump off the seat. Alternatively, attach a swivel hook to your pet's harness, and use a short piece of rope or a shoelace to tie the harness securely to the seat belt (see photo). Belting up your ferret is practical only for short trips. After all, how could he get at his litter box, food dish, and water bowl? And, belting up is practical only for some ferrets—those easy riders that will sit quietly or doze off during the trip. For restless riders, stick to the carriers or cages.

A small travel carrier is fine for short trips but too cramped for long journeys. So, when vacation time rolls around, your pet will be more comfortable in an extra large carrier or a good-sized cage where he'll have all the comforts of home at his paw tips. To make sure the cage or carrier is secure in the car, slot a seat belt through the wires or top handle. This will prevent it from becoming a missile or a free-flying object in the event you have to stop suddenly.

A ferret seat belt . . .

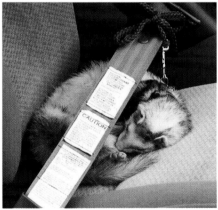

. . . keeps your pet from roaming around the car.

Most ferrets adapt to car travel well, especially if you get them used to the car first. Start by taking short trips around the block, then gradually increase the length of the trips. However, some ferrets are not good travelers. Do you have a compulsive clawer that scratches frantically to get out of that carrier? A few miles of this and you'll be frantic, too. Can you do anything about obsessive scratchers? Unfortunately, not a lot. Some may cease and desist when the scratching gets them nowhere— so ignoring it is worth a try. If that doesn't work, a lengthy and energetic exercise session before departure might wear him out enough so that he snoozes on the journey. Your only other options are to buy earplugs or to leave your scratcher at home, because you can't teach a determined ferret to stop clawing.

Here's a car travel alert. Ferrets and hot cars don't mix. Because ferrets are very prone to heatstroke, it's dangerous to put your pet into a hot car or ferry him around in one. Don't be fooled by cooler temperatures—if the sun is beating down on the car windows, the car interior will heat up like a greenhouse. No air-conditioning in your vehicle? Then leave your ferret home on hot days. Or, if a visit to the vet is necessary, keep your fuzzy cool with cold packs or ice cubes in Ziplock bags. These can be wrapped in towels and placed into the pet carrier beside your passenger.

Vacation Time

Is it time to plan for your next vacation? Are you thinking of including your furry sidekick in your plans? Think carefully. Where are you going, and what are you going to be doing? Is it practical for your pal to tag along? A trip to the big city for wining, dining, museum hopping, and theater going will be fun for you,

Secured on a leash, Sherlock's included in the family vacation.

but what fun will it be for your ferret? While you're out painting the town, he'll be stuck back in the hotel room, moping, sulking, or scratching. Maybe you enjoy lounging at the beach, but the beach is not the best place for ferrets—swallowing sand or salt water and trotting across a burning beach is *not* in your pet's best interest. However, if you're having a week's R&R in a mountain cabin, by all means bring your furball along to enjoy some R&R of his own.

If your plans include visiting the relatives, is your ferret included in the invitation? Not all people are pet lovers. Or, if they are pet lovers, the big dog they love might not take to the furry friend you love. So never show up at your nearest and dearest with a ferret surprise . . . or the visit might be surprisingly short.

Then there's the question of temperature. When the mercury soars above 80°F (27°C), it's too hot for your ferret to handle. Remember, ferrets can die if they get over-heated. Your ferret might enjoy a camping trip in cool weather but not if a heat wave is forecast.

The bottom line is, you have to be sensible when figuring your ferret into your travel plans. Every ferret, every owner, every travel situation is different—only you can decide if it's a smart move to take your buddy along.

Protocol for Visiting Furballs

Wherever you're taking your ferret, whether it's to a relative's house, a hotel or motel, a cabin in the woods, or a condo at the lake, there are certain guidelines that you should follow. These guidelines will ensure that your ferret is a well-behaved guest. But more importantly, they will ensure his safety.

For example, when you reach your destination, you can't just throw open the travel cage door and say, "Out you come . . . we're here!" Have you forgotten about the ferret proofing? After all, think of what your ferret might find in a quick tour of your sister's living room or in an efficiency motel's kitchen cupboards. So, in any vacation accommodation, free roam is out and leash control is in. That is, whenever your ferret's out of his travel cage, he should be wearing his harness and leash, and the leash should be in your hand. Or, if you've ferret proofed the area around the travel carrier, why not tie the leash to the top of the carrier and let your traveler stretch his legs?

Another option is to ferret proof a bathroom so that your furry friend can have a bit of leash-free, supervised freedom. But don't go this route unless you can absolutely guarantee his safety. The bathroom also comes in handy at bedtime, especially in a hotel/motel situation. You can stash the cage, complete with ferret, in there at nighttime so that your beauty sleep won't be disturbed if your night owl rustles, scratches, chomps, or slurps during the wee hours of the morning.

Safety issues are important but so are courtesy issues. Always make sure in advance that your pet will be a welcome guest, whether you're staying with relatives or at paid accommodations. Not all hotels permit pets—and those that do may be thinking along the lines of cats and dogs rather than ferrets. Make advance reservations, and be specific about the type of pet you're bringing.

When away from home, your ferret could be a little less particular about his litter box habits. He won't leave a very good impression if he starts dropping little poop piles in the corners. So be vigilant. Make sure he gets to the box in time, every time. If, heaven forbid, he misses the box, clean up the accident right away with the pet deodorizer you packed.

One plus that makes a ferret a good houseguest is that he's *usually* seen and not heard—no woofing, no yowling, no screeching. But what if you have a cage scratcher that drives everybody nuts? That annoying habit will certainly put a return invitation in jeopardy. Is there anything you can do about it? Look at the situation from your ferret's point of view. He's in a strange place, he's probably cooped up more than usual, and he wants out to explore. So, the best way to tackle the annoying clawing is to give your pet a tour of his new surroundings and get him out for regular exercise sessions during the day, especially before bedtime. A tuckered-out ferret is more likely to crash than to claw.

Rules and Regulations

You can't always pick up and go with a ferret as you would with a dog or a cat. Ferrets are illegal in some places. Certain states, cities, and towns are designated ferret-free zones. Other states and municipalities require that you have a ferret license or an exotics' license, even if you're just passing through. It's impossible to give a listing of what places have what restrictions, because regulations and bylaws are constantly changing. The onus is on you to contact the appropriate authorities, to find out what, if any, restrictions apply, and to complete any necessary paperwork. How do you know who to call? The answer isn't cut and dried. Depending on your travel itinerary, you might have to contact a federal department, a state agency, a provincial ministry, or a municipal office. You might even need to get in touch with all of the above. Or check the Internet for information, keeping in mind that not everything you read on the Net is current and up-to-date.

Will your ferret be border hopping with you? Call the Customs offices on both sides of the border, find out what documentation is needed, and—most importantly—get the information in writing. Be aware, too, that when you're crossing from Canada into the United States, it's not only the federal regulations that you need to find out about. You also have to check into the state regulations at your point of entry as well as the regulations for every state you plan to travel through. This may seem like going to extremes. However, if you're asked at the border about your destination and you don't have the appropriate licenses, permits, or documentation, you could find yourself heading home instead of to the sunny South. Rules are rules, and border officials won't make an exception in your case. Whatever you do, never try to smuggle your furball—the possible consequences aren't worth it.

No matter where you're traveling, always take along your ferret's vaccination record (rabies and distemper shots) and a recent health certificate from your veterinarian. And talking about veterinarians, one of the first things to do when arriving

Can you believe there are ferret-free zones?

at your destination is to check the yellow pages for veterinarians who specialize in ferrets or in exotic pets. This is a safety precaution in case a medical emergency arises.

Flying the friendly skies might not always be a fuzzy-friendly experience. With different airlines having different rules and regulations, it's difficult to generalize about ferret travel. It's up to you to contact the individual airlines well in advance of your travel date and ask these questions: Does the airline allow ferrets onto the plane? If so, can they travel in the cabin with you, or are they consigned to cargo? (Cargo travel is not recommended—your pet's life could be in danger if he has to wait outside for boarding in very hot or very cold weather. Also, the noise in the cargo hold is not ferret friendly.) Is a special type of travel carrier mandatory? Is there an extra cost involved? Is a veterinarian exam required before travel? When you get answers, get them in writing so that there won't be any misunderstandings at the check-in counter at flight time.

The Stay-at-Home Ferret

Sometimes it's neither fair nor feasible to take your ferret traveling. For example, if your pet is very hyper or excitable, why put him through the stresses and strains of travel? Or, if you're planning an activity-packed vacation, when will you have time to look after your ferret? In either case, it's probably better to leave your buddy behind. Don't feel guilty about leaving your furball—just make sure he's left in good hands.

Sometimes it's possible to leave him right in his own home environment with a ferret baby-sitter. Does a dear friend or a close relative owe you big time? Now's the time to call in the favor. Can you convince (or pay) your friend to come into the house at least twice a day to check on food and water and to play with your pal? In your own home, your ferret will be relaxed and at ease— more importantly, he'll be safe because you've seen to the ferret proofing. Although his daily routine may be disrupted, at least he's in familiar surroundings. When family and friends don't live close enough for this arrangement to work, check your local newspaper or yellow pages for a professional pet-sitting service. For a fee, you can have someone visit your pet twice a day to provide care and exercise.

Do family or friends live too far away? Is pet sitting too expensive or not available where you live? Then you'll have to forget in-home care and look instead at boarding-out options. You have several choices here. Perhaps that friend or relative who couldn't come to your house will be happy to give your darling a home away from home while you're gone. Or, if you live in an area where's there an active ferret club, check to see if any of the members do ferret sitting. This would be an excellent option because club members know all the ins and outs of ferret care. And who knows? Maybe you could work out a swap system where you exchange ferret-sitting favors without money changing hands.

Boarding kennels are another possibility. Not all kennels are strictly for dogs or cats—call around to find out which ones are ferret friendly. Then it's time for a visit and inspection. Is the place clean? Do the animals look well cared for? Would the staff be comfortable handling your ferret? Could a noise-sensitive ferret be kept well away from barking dogs? Can you check references? Time spent scrutinizing the facilities is time well spent—you'll be able to enjoy your own holiday without worrying about your ferret's well-being.

Some veterinary clinics offer boarding services. This is a particularly good alternative if you have a sick, elderly, or frail ferret. Does your own vet offer this service? Then you're in luck—the staff already knows your pet. Your animal clinic doesn't offer boarding services? Ask the staff to recommend a veterinary facility that does. You might find, however, that the cost of care at a veterinary clinic is a little higher than the cost of care at other boarding facilities.

Whether you're going to leave your pet behind in his own home or in a home away from home, be sure to write a list of important information for the caregiver. Include
• telephone numbers where you can be reached in case of an emergency
• your veterinarian's phone number and the number of the nearest ferret-friendly, after-hours emergency clinic
• details about feeding and treats
• exercise requirements
• an adequate supply of any necessary medications and precise details on how to administer them
• information and instructions to ensure your ferret's safety, for example, no free roaming in an area not ferret proofed

It's also important to have a heart-to-heart discussion with the caregiver about the steps to take if there's a ferret medical emergency and you can't be reached. Is the caregiver to do whatever's necessary to save the ferret's life? Or, is there a limit to the amount of money you can afford to spend? If so, what course of action is the caregiver to take?

It doesn't matter whether you're taking your ferret with you or leaving him at home. Either way, advance planning is necessary—your pet is your responsibility.

Chapter Thirteen
Grooming

Bath Time

Have you noticed a hint of musk in the air lately? Or, does the smell of ferret B.O. bowl you over when you walk in the door? Then it's time, or past time, for the fuzzy to have a scrub in the tub.

Unfortunately, your buddy won't come begging for a bath. In fact, if she gets wind of what's afoot, she'll turn tail and hightail it out of sight and out of reach. Most ferrets don't like baths. So here are some suggestions to keep odor at bay and bath times to a minimum. First and foremost, make sure your pet is spayed or neutered. This will take care of 90 percent of a ferret's musky odor. Next, feed your fuzzy high-quality ferret food. A ferret that eats poor-quality food produces more poop, and the poop is more smelly. Also, be persnickety about those litter boxes—daily scoop patrol is necessary. Finally, keep your ferret's cage and bedding clean, clean, clean. Take these steps, and you'll go a long way toward reducing that familiar ferret fragrance.

Just how often should a ferret have a bath? There are no hard-and-fast rules—a lot depends on how fastidious you are and how fragrant your ferret is. Some ferrets have a stronger odor and greasier fur than others, and the smell can vary according to the age and health of your pet. So let your nose be the guide. However, don't overdo the weasel washes or you'll dry out your ferret's skin and strip her fur of oils. Never give your ferret a bath more than once a week, and once or twice a month is probably nearer the mark.

When bath time does roll around, it's a good idea to wait until your ferret's used her litter box. Accidents can happen in the bath water, and it's a mess to clean up. It's also best to keep your ferret in her cage while you get things ready or your ferret will clue in quickly to the bath routine and make herself scarce. Line up shampoo, conditioner, and towel, run an inch or two (2.5 to 5 cm) of warm water into the tub or a sink—*then* fetch the ferret.

While speaking reassuringly, lower her into the water and hold her there with one hand so she can't go AWOL. With the other hand, wet her

Squeaky clean.

fur. Then squeeze a ribbon of ferret, kitten, or tearless baby shampoo along her back and rub-a-dub-dub. Now squeeze some shampoo onto tummy and tail. Lather well. There are a few areas that need special attention because of skin secretions—the chin, the top of the nose, the back of the neck, and the tail all need an extra-good scrub. Be careful, though . . . don't get soap into her eyes, into her ears, or up her nose. And work fast. Lots of ferrets like the taste of shampoo, and they'll lick, lick, lick until they get sick, sick, sick.

As soon as your water baby's squeaky clean, rinse her well, either in several changes of water or under warm (not hot) running water. A spray attachment comes in handy here. Every trace of shampoo must go down the drain or your ferret's skin will itch. Now finish to salon standards by using a ferret coat conditioner to give your fuzzy's fur that soft, silky feel. Conditioners made specifically for ferrets usually contain a deodorizer, too, that helps with odor control. Again, rinse well. You could also make a homemade rinse by adding a teaspoon (5 ml) of apple-cider vinegar to a sink of water. Swish your pet around in the rinse—it will restore her normal skin pH balance and leave her smelling fresh.

After the final rinse, *gently* squeeze your ferret all over to remove excess water. Then wrap her in a large, fluffy towel. About this time, you'll notice that your ferret's flipped on the hyper switch. For some reason, most ferrets go into an absolute frenzy after a bath. So, the trick with the towel is to keep her in it long enough to dry her off. Holding her against your chest or sitting down with her on your lap are two ways to get a good grip. Hang on tight, and rub briskly until she's almost dry (or until you can't hold on any longer).

Now the fun begins. Watch that baby go! After a bath, your ferret knows only one gear, and that's high gear. She'll race around, roll about, rub against everything and anything, dart under furniture, bounce off the walls, drag her bottom along the carpet—in other words, go nuts. Let her go; she's having fun. And don't put her back into her cage or she'll most likely roll around in her litter box . . . just what you don't want after bath time.

In the midst of all the scooting and scurrying, she'll stop every so often for a bout of frenzied fur licking. While sitting back on her haunches, she'll get busy licking her bottom, too. What she's doing is completing her grooming, finishing off to ferret standards. But all of this licking can cause hairballs, so make furball prevention part of the bath routine. Give her about a 0.5-inch (1.3 cm) to a 1-inch (2.5 cm) ribbon of furball medicine after every bath. Most ferrets love this stuff, so it can double as a reward for being *such* a good girl.

Some ferrets that fuss about a sink bath feel more comfortable paddling around in the tub, and some that are intimidated by the tub feel more secure in the sink. However, if your fuzzy kicks up her heels about any kind of bath, try taking her into the shower with you. Just watch out for toe attacks; showering ferrets sometimes forget that toe nipping is a no-no.

Do you have an elderly, frail, or sick ferret? It might be better to use some dry ferret shampoo rather than to put her through the stress of bath time. Don't sprinkle the dry stuff directly onto your ferret; you don't want clouds of dust irritating her eyes and being breathed up her nose. Instead, sprinkle the powder into your hand and then rub it gently into your ferret's fur. Do you have a flea-infested ferret? See Chapter 15 for information on using flea shampoos.

You may not be able to make bath time fun time for your fuzzy, but you can at least make it as fright-free as possible. Never let the water get hotter than warm . . . if it's too hot for your wrist, it's too hot for your ferret. Never leave your pet alone in the tub or sink . . .not even to answer the phone. She could drown in the bath or injure herself jumping out of the sink. And use a hair dryer only at a low setting and only if your bathing beauty can stand the noise . . . the noise scares most ferrets.

Ear Cleaning

If your ferret's not too fond of bath time, it's a safe bet she'll like ear cleaning even less. However, whether she likes it or not, ferret ears need to be cleaned regularly to

I'm ready for action after my bath.

Cotton swabs work well for ear cleaning, just don't poke them in too far.

take care of the reddish brown wax that builds up in them. Unfortunately, ear cleaning presents problems. Not many self-respecting ferrets welcome cotton swabs with a smile. So a little cunning and bribery may be needed if you're to get the job done.

First, set up your supplies—ferret ear cleaner and five or six cotton swabs. Then bring the ear cleaner to body temperature by rubbing the bottle between your palms, holding it against your body, or placing it into a cup of warm water. If you drop cold liquid into your fuzzy's ears, she won't like it. In fact, you might never get the stuff into her ears again.

Next, squeeze a few drops of cleaner into one ear, and massage gently to loosen the wax in the ear canal. Your ferret will most likely shake her head, which helps to bring

the wax to the outer ear. This is where the cotton swabs come in. Moisten one end of a swab with ear cleaner, and carefully wipe out the folds and crevices in the outer ear. You'll be amazed at the amount of junk you'll collect! Use as many swabs as necessary to get rid of all the debris. Then do the next ear.

Sounds easy, doesn't it? But if your ferret is putting up a fight, it's anything but easy. Resort to bribery! A few drops of Ferretone, Ferret Derm, Furo-Tone, Linatone, or the like on your ferret's tummy should divert her attention long enough for you to get the job done. Another ploy is to attempt ear cleaning while your ferret's sleeping. Remember, ferrets sleep very soundly, so this isn't as impossible as it sounds. You may, however, have to do the two ears at two separate times if the sleepyhead wakes up before the job is finished.

A really difficult ferret can be scruffed for ear cleaning. Take hold of the loose skin at the back of her neck, and lift her gently so that she's dangling vertically. Rest her hind legs on a table or your lap. Scruffing causes a ferret to go limp, and this in turn makes her more manageable during ear cleaning. A helper could also be handy here—while one of you scruffs, the other can clean.

When cleaning ears, be careful not to stab those swabs into the ear canal. And be gentle. Ears are sensitive. If you once hurt your ferret, she'll think twice about letting you tamper with her ears again.

It won't take long to get used to the ear-cleaning routine. You'll soon become familiar with every crease and crevice in your ferret's ears. If, however, you notice anything unusual, such as excessive amounts of reddish brown wax, blackish wax, strong-smelling wax, or any discharge from the ears, make an appointment for your pet to see the vet. Any of these signs could mean ear mites or infection.

Toenail Clipping

Ouch! Wow, those ferret nails are sharp! It's no surprise . . . ferret nails grow like human nails, only with sharp points. If you don't trim them regularly, playtime could be a scratchy business. And let's face it, getting scratched by a long ferret dagger isn't much fun. In addition, your ferret could get her long nails caught and ripped on bedding, in carpets, or on your clothing. She won't be happy, and you won't appreciate the resulting snags in sweaters, sofas, or comforters. Long nails also make it more difficult for a ferret to walk properly. If you let ferret nails grow too long, the blood vein that goes through the nail (the quick) will grow long, too. Then you won't be able to cut the nails short in the future because you should never cut through the quick. So, with all things taken into consideration, regular toenail trimming for your ferret is a must.

How often is regular? This could be anywhere from once a week to once a month, depending on how fast the nails grow and whether or not your ferret's wearing them down on hard walking surfaces. The best plan is to check the nails once a week and trim them when necessary.

Get off to a good start by getting the right kind of clipper. Cat claw clippers are best, though some owners find that toenail clippers made for people do a good job, too. The main thing is to buy good-quality clippers. It's false economy to buy a cheap pair that will quickly blunt and rip the nail rather than making a clean cut. Don't buy guillotine-style clippers because they don't stay sharp and it's hard to see exactly where and what you're cutting.

The best way to get nail trimming done is to wait until your ferret's sound asleep. Sit down in a comfortable chair under a good light, rest your ferret in your lap, and do

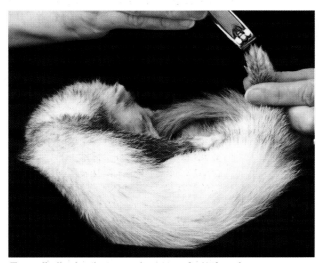

Toenail clipping is easy when your ferret's asleep.

the sleep test. Lift up one paw, and let it go. If it drops and there's no response, your furball's fast asleep. Did you get a reaction from your fuzzy? Then wait a bit longer until she's definitely out for the count before starting the manicure. The trick is to take your time. If your ferret stirs when you're only on the third toe, stop. Wait a while until she drifts off again before tackling the next couple of toes.

When you don't have time for the sleep trick, or when your kit doesn't cooperate, try bribery again. Bring out the Ferretone, and anoint that tummy. Then, while your ferret's busy licking, you get busy clipping. Add more Ferretone as necessary until the job is done.

Does your ferret pull her paws back whenever the clippers get near them? Perhaps you need to enlist a helper. One of you can scruff the ferret while the other clips her nails.

Whatever trimming tactic works, that's the one you want to go with. And when you do get down to business, good lighting is very important. You need to be able to see properly so that you can avoid cutting the quick. The quick shows up as a reddish pink line going through the nail lengthwise. It's reddish pink because it's a blood vessel. If you cut into it, it will bleed. Worse yet, it will hurt like heck and your ferret won't forgive and forget. Cut a quick and you'll certainly have future battles at nail trimming time. So always make sure you snip above the quick. However, accidents can happen. In case you

do nick the quick, it's a good idea to have a styptic pencil on hand to stop the bleeding. No styptic pencils in the house? Cornstarch will work. Pour some onto your palm, and dip the injured toenail into it.

After the nails have been cut, smooth any rough or ragged edges with an emery board. This helps prevent the nail from catching on material and being ripped out accidentally.

Are you squeamish about toenail duty? It might help to have your veterinarian give you a step-by-step demonstration. Or, if there's a ferret club in your area, a friendly club member might be willing to give you private lessons. Is your ferret positively pigheaded about pedicures? Check the prices at the poodle parlor—ask if they'll do ferret feet.

One last word on ferret toenails. Leave them where they're meant to be—on ferret feet. NEVER, NEVER, NEVER have your ferret declawed. Ferret claws are not retractable like a cat's; they grow like a dog's. Declawing is painful and actually mutilates a ferret's paws. It also affects normal daily activities like walking, climbing, digging, gripping, and playing. Don't do it.

Paw Pads

Make paw pad care a regular part of your pet's pedicure. Check your ferret's paw pads several times a week. Do they look dry or scaly? Do they feel rough or leathery? Ferrets of all ages, but especially older fuzzies, can get dry feet. Dryness can also be a problem for ferrets that use clay litter and for those that pound the pavement on a daily basis.

The solution's simple—just massage a drop or two of vitamin E oil or good-quality hand lotion into each foot pad. Make sure you rub it in completely so that your ferret can't lick it off or track oily prints all over your floors or carpets. Be diligent about moisturizing, and it won't be long before those rough, dry pads become soft and supple. Your ferret will have a new spring in her step.

If you notice anything unusual about your pet's foot pads—such as bleeding, cracking, swelling, thickening, or bruising—consult your veterinarian. There could be a medical problem that needs attention.

Coat and Skin Conditioners

Not all ferret fur has the same feel. Some ferrets have long, soft, silky fur. Others have short, coarse, woolly-feeling fur. Some ferrets have thick, luxurious coats, while others have thinner, sparser coats. And, the same ferret can have a thicker or a thinner coat depending on the time of year. Whatever type of coat your pet has, your job as an owner is to keep it in tip-top condition.

Good nutrition is essential for healthy fur and skin. Ferrets need a

Paw pads can get cracked and dry. Use moisturizer to keep them in A-1 condition.

particular balance of high-quality animal protein and fat in their diet. If your ferret's fur is looking flat and lifeless, the first thing you need to do is review her diet. Is she getting the nutrition she needs? Go back and reread Chapter 4.

For supple skin and glossy fur, oil-based fatty acid supplements are highly recommended for ferrets. Look for Ferret Derm, Ferretone, Furo-Tone, Linatone for ferrets, Pet Derm, and Vet's Best Healthy Coat Supplement, for example. A small amount of a fatty acid supplement daily will add luster to your pet's coat. This is one aspect of ferret care that your fuzzy won't rebel against. Most ferrets love the stuff, but never give more than the recommended amount—read the package directions carefully.

Fatty acid supplements work from the inside; other skin and coat conditioners work from the outside. Try after-shampoo cream rinses or spray-on conditioners to nourish the skin, shine up the fur, and beat ferret B.O.

After all of this skin and coat care, does your fuzzy still itch and scratch? Some ferrets seem to be naturally itchy. When they wake up, their scratching can shake the cage. However, if you notice your ferret scratching excessively or biting at her skin, she could be suffering from fleas or allergies, she could be getting her new spring or winter coat, or she could have an undiagnosed medical problem. When in doubt, visit the vet.

For healthy skin and a shiny coat, include fatty acid supplements in your ferret's diet.

Your furball's getting a top-notch diet, she's getting daily fatty acid supplements, and she's just been given a clean bill of health at the vet's—but her coat still seems thin, dull, and dry? Is there anything you've missed? Check the thermostat. You may be a hothouse plant, but ferrets are uncomfortable when the house temperature tops 80°F (27°C). If you suspect that high heat in the house is causing your pet's poor coat quality, turn the thermostat down. If low humidity could be the culprit, buy a room humidifier.

Brushing and Plucking

Brush, brush, brush. Brush, brush, brush. No, it's not you getting ready for a big night on the town. And, no . . . your ferret's not getting ready for her shot at Best of Show. All this brushing is just part and parcel of your regular ferret grooming routine. Taking care of your ferret's fur is more than a beauty treatment; it serves a practical purpose, too. Brushing helps to remove loose hair that your ferret might otherwise lick and swallow. Too much ingested hair can form hairballs. These, in turn, can cause internal blockage because ferrets can't cough them up. So it's a good idea to get into the habit of brushing your furball several times a week. This way, you'll be the one taking care of the loose hair problem instead of leaving it up to your ferret.

Is it spring cleaning time? Have you noticed extra clumps of ferret fur mingling with the dust bunnies? That's because it's ferret shedding time. Ferrets usually have two major shedding periods a year, one in spring and one in fall. In the spring, they shed their thick winter coat and get a sleek summer coat. In the fall, dead hair from their summer coat falls out so that the thick winter coat can grow in again. When shedding, your pet will lose much more hair than usual—just stroking her will often bring out handfuls of hair. However, ferrets that spend most of their time indoors at a fairly constant temperature and in typical household lighting conditions don't have such a pronounced difference between their winter and summer coats, and the shedding periods might not be so predictable. You'll be able to tell when the shedding starts, and when it does, be very diligent about brushing. Do it daily.

Brushing doesn't require much equipment. All you need is a ferret brush, a ball-tipped bristle brush, a soft cat brush, or a pet grooming glove. For a really thorough job, a flea comb works well. Choose brushing time carefully—a playful ferret's not going to sit still for a beauty makeover. So wait until playtime's over if you want a cooperative customer. Then get out the brush and start brushing—in the direction of fur growth, please.

Some ferrets love to be brushed. They'll lie there totally relaxed and will even let you massage them with

Brushing takes care of loose hair that could cause hairballs.

the brush. Other ferrets hate the hairbrush, and it's a real challenge to get the job done. When you have a hairdo hater on your hands, wait till she's having forty winks before you begin brushing. And don't drag out the styling session. When your ferret starts fussing, get in a few more brush strokes so that she knows she has to grin and bear it, then let her go. If you put her down the moment *she* wants down, she'll quickly learn that fussing and fidgeting gets her what she wants—not a lesson you want to encourage.

Try to make brushing time fun time for both of you. If you start the salon sessions when your ferret's a kit, keep them up on a regular basis, and throw in treats every so often, the brushing sessions shouldn't be so hairy for either of you.

Brushing isn't the only solution when shedding time rolls around.

Plucking that ferret is another possibility. Plucking??? What's that? It's holding your fuzzy over a wastebasket and quickly (but gently) tugging out tufts of loose hair all over her body. You should do this *only* during shedding periods and *only* when the fur comes out easily—fur that's pluck resistant isn't ready to come out yet. Proper plucking is painless, and it's a good way to get the dead fur directly into the garbage. Just think of the vacuuming time you'll save—time that can be better spent cavorting with your ferret.

When shedding time rolls around, plucking your pet gets rid of loose hair . . . fast.

Plucking can give your ferret a somewhat scraggly appearance . . . for a short time anyway. But don't worry, the skimpy patches will soon fill out as the hair grows in. And while you're waiting for the new coat to come in, don't be alarmed if you notice that the skin of your dark-colored ferret has a distinct bluish or khaki cast to it that wasn't there before. This discoloration is perfectly normal just before new fur starts growing in.

When you're brushing your pet, keep your eyes peeled. Unusual hair loss, bald spots, skin changes, lumps, bumps, or anything else out of the ordinary warrants a call to your veterinarian.

Toothbrushing Tips

To keep your ferret's smile beaming, you'll have to pay attention to her teeth. Unfortunately, most pet owners don't realize that their pets need tooth care. Even when a ferret eats high-quality dry ferret food, she accumulates plaque and tartar on her teeth. When the soft, gummy plaque isn't removed, it turns into hard tartar. When the hard tartar isn't removed, it leads to tooth decay and gum disease. Good dental hygiene will keep plaque under control and minimize tartar buildup.

So, the first thing you need to do is get a toothbrush for your fuzzy. A child's toothbrush or one made specifically for small pets should do the trick. But the biggest trick is getting the toothbrush into your ferret's mouth. If you start toothbrushing when your ferret's a kit, she'll be less likely to rebel. What can you do, however, if you have a ferret that clamps those lips shut? Try gentle restraint. Flip her onto her back on your lap, then hold her head while you get the job done. Massaging the area below her ears at the jaw hinge will cause her to yawn and make it easier to get the brush in. Or, support her on your lap and scruff her. Scruffing leads to yawning, and yawning gives you the opportunity to get at a few teeth. Still having difficulties? Sneak in a few brush strokes while she's asleep.

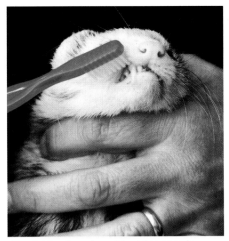

Dental hygiene is not just for people.

Be gentle when cleaning your ferret's teeth. Brush with an up-and-down motion—not too vigorously and not for too long. A minute or two daily or every couple of days is better than a five-minute session once a month. Always dampen the brush with water; pet toothpaste is optional.

Realize that you won't be able to do the same job on your ferret's teeth as you do on your own. Forget the dental floss—and don't be surprised if you can't get right in to the back teeth or even to the inside of the front teeth. A lot depends on what your ferret will tolerate. So the rule of thumb is do what you can. Then have your veterinarian examine your pet's teeth at every scheduled health checkup. As your ferret ages, she may need a thorough dental scaling by the vet once or twice a year. This is done under general anesthetic. *Never* try scraping your pet's teeth yourself—she's liable to shake her head or clamp down on the dental scaler. In either case, the pointy end of the tool could stab her, or she could break a tooth.

Chapter Fourteen

Special-Need Ferrets Are Special Too!

Handicapped? Who . . . Me?

Due to age, illness, injury, or congenital factors, some ferrets are—or become—blind or deaf. But ferrets don't know the meaning of the word handicapped. Even if they have physical disabilities, they find a way to live life to the fullest. Although adaptation is the name of their game, you can make life easier for these "special-need" ferrets by giving them special consideration when it comes to handling and training.

Vision-Impaired Ferrets

Even ferrets with normal vision have difficulty making out far-away objects, but there's absolutely nothing wrong with their close-up vision. This clear close-up vision combined with a fantastic sense of smell gets the normal-sighted ferret around any household environment with ease. It's not quite so easy for blind ferrets to get around, but, fortunately, they quickly learn to adapt to their surroundings.

How can you tell that your ferret's having difficulty seeing? Observe her behavior carefully. Does she bump into things that she detoured around before? Does she have trouble negotiating steps? Does she trip over the shoes you left in the hallway? And, does she barrel right into the sofa you moved in the family room? When a ferret collides with things, refuses to come out of her cage, acts startled when picked up, or becomes aggressive toward other pets in the house, suspect vision problems.

A resident fuzzy should be able to take loss or impairment of vision in her stride. After all, she's been living in the house and knows where everything is. As long as you don't move things, she shouldn't skip a beat. However, don't go rearranging the furniture on her, closing doors that are usually open, or cluttering up her floor space.

To avoid frightening a blind ferret, always speak to her before picking her up—a frightened ferret is more likely to nip or bite. And talk to her more frequently so she knows where you are in the room.

For a blind newcomer, all of the above advice applies. In addition, you might have to do some extra ferret proofing, like barricading railings and stairs. You'll also have to teach the newbie the layout of her play space. She'll want to walk alongside the walls at first, but encourage her to venture into the open as she feels more confident. Pay particular attention to changes in level—you might have to help her negotiate steps. Don't just plop her on the steps one at a time. Take her paws and physically walk her up the steps so that she learns to navigate them herself.

Blind ferrets seem to have an uncanny ability to adapt to their surroundings. Before you know it, your furball will have the whole floor plan committed to memory and will be scooting around just fine.

When a blind ferret's not an only ferret, watch carefully to see how she interacts with her ferret buddies. If she's startled when approached, she might nip as a defensive reaction. Outfitting the rest of the bunch with bells (on collar or harness) will let her know when they're coming. She might even dub one buddy her "guide ferret" and play follow the leader to get around.

Deaf Ferrets

Deaf ferrets, like blind ones, need special consideration. Never rush up behind a deaf ferret and scoop her up—think how startled you'd be if you couldn't hear and someone rushed up behind you. Always approach a deaf ferret from the front so she can see you coming. And always approach her slowly. Try getting her attention by hand waving or floor knocking. Some deaf ferrets can feel the vibrations of a wooden

Ferrets don't let vision impairment hold them down.

When a ferret's hearing impaired, you'll have to modify your training techniques.

floor even though they can't hear the knocking.

Hearing-impaired ferrets don't, of course, respond to the use of the word "No!" in training. Scruffing is usually much more effective. Look directly into the eyes of the dangling scruffee, and shake your head back and forth as a form of discipline. Don't feel foolish if you find yourself saying the words "No, no, no!" automatically. Who knows? Your ferret may learn to lip read!

To make up for the fact that you can't caress a deaf ferret with the sound of your voice, cuddle her close and give her extras hugs and kisses. Talk to her, too. She won't know what you're saying, but when held close, she'll be able to feel the vibrations of your chest as you talk. Many ferrets that are hard of hearing find the closeness comforting and the vibration soothing.

Because ferrets with hearing loss don't react to loud noises, they can tolerate situations that might frighten other ferrets. For example, a ferret with good hearing will often be rattled by the rumble of trucks, while a hearing-impaired ferret will wander around without a worry in the world.

Many deaf ferrets are more vocal than their hearing counterparts. Does your deaf ferret scream while playing? Don't be concerned. She's probably not hurt, just vocalizing her joy.

Chapter Fifteen
Health Concerns

Taking Health Care to Heart

When you flip through the pages of this chapter, you might be a bit taken aback at its length. Don't worry—not everything you read about is something your ferret's going to come down with! Don't think, either, that the information provided here is a substitute for qualified medical diagnosis and/or treatment. There is no substitute for a veterinarian when your pet is ill. Rather, the purpose of this chapter is to give you an overview in layperson's terms of common ferret ailments so that you can keep a watchful eye on your ferret's health.

After all, you're the one who's living with your fuzzy day to day; you're the one who's going to notice right away if any change occurs in his appearance or behavior. Should you notice anything unusual, don't try to play doctor yourself. Symptoms for many ferret diseases and illnesses are similar—it takes a ferret-knowledgeable veterinarian to make a proper diagnosis. And, don't postpone a needed visit to the vet-

erinarian. Ferrets are small animals. If you adopt a wait-and-see attitude, a sick one can go downhill quickly without appropriate medical care.

Finding a Ferret-Knowledgeable Veterinarian

When it's time to visit the vet, it's important to find one who knows about ferrets. If you break a leg, you wouldn't run off to a heart specialist for treatment, would you? So if your ferret gets sick, why would you want him seen by a cat specialist or a dog specialist? The fact of the matter is not all veterinarians know more than the basics about ferrets, and some won't even take on ferrets as patients.

Why do you need a ferret-knowledgeable veterinarian? In the first place, when it comes time for your fuzzy's annual immunizations, you want a vet who knows which vaccines to administer and what to do in the event of an allergic reaction (see following section). Even more important, you want a veterinarian

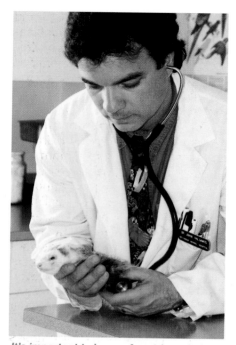

It's important to have a ferret-knowledge-able veterinarian for your pet.

who knows what to look for when doing the annual examination that should accompany the inoculations. For that ferret physical, would you prefer a vet who has examined a hundred ferrets or a vet who has examined two ferrets? Would you prefer a vet who knows immediately that your ferret's spleen is enlarged or a vet who doesn't know what size a ferret's spleen should be anyway?

However, it's not just for physicals and vaccinations that you want a ferret-savvy veterinarian. If your ferret gets sick, a veterinarian experienced with ferrets is much more likely to come up with the right diagnosis quickly so that treatment can

be started promptly. Different ferret illnesses or diseases can present with the same symptoms—experience saves time. Especially in the case of an emergency, having a ferret specialist could mean the difference between life and death for your pet.

The best time to find a ferret veterinarian is before you buy that furball. OOPS—already got the fuzzy? Then, the second best time to find the right vet is right now. Do *not* wait until your pet has a problem. Get on the ball now, and get a good vet. Call around to different clinics and ask the following questions:
• Is there a vet in the practice who is experienced in treating ferrets?
• How many ferret patients are in the practice?
• Is the veterinarian knowledgeable about vaccinations for ferrets?
• Has the vet done any surgeries on ferrets?
• Does the clinic offer after-hours emergency service? If not, where do you go in an emergency?

What happens when you call every clinic in town and there's not a ferret specialist to be found? Ask other ferret owners in your area where they take their pets. Check with local ferret clubs for a list of ferret-friendly veterinarians in your state or province. Get on the Internet and surf to Ferret Central—here you'll find links to sites that will give you listings. Or, call the nearest school of veterinary medicine and ask for recommendations. Realize that you might have to travel a distance for the quality care your ferret requires.

Next problem—when pets get sick, it never seems to happen on a Wednesday morning when your veterinary clinic's open for business. Oh, no! Emergencies always seem to happen on Saturday nights at bedtime, when office hours are long since over. Some veterinary clinics take care of their own after-hours emergencies with on-call service. Does yours? If not, what do they advise? Do they recommend a local emergency clinic? Please be forewarned that not all after-hours clinics will agree to see ferrets in a medical emergency. Not all vets have been trained in ferret medicine, and some vets don't feel comfortable dealing with ferrets. You may have to travel to another town in order to obtain emergency care for your pet.

Whatever arrangements you end up making for after-hours emergency care, this point can't be overstressed—you must know exactly where you're going to take your pet in an emergency so that you don't waste valuable time. Keep all telephone numbers for emergency care in a handy place . . . there's nothing worse than having a very sick pet and not being able to find the right phone number for the right clinic when you need it.

Immunizations

Your ferret's first visit to the veterinarian will probably be for immunization shots. Ferrets, like dogs and cats, need to have yearly vaccinations to ward off potentially life-threatening diseases. Vaccinations fall under the heading of preventative health care. They're very important for your pet's well-being.

Ferrets should be immunized against rabies. Rabies is a viral illness transmitted from mammal to mammal by saliva, usually by a bite from an infected animal. Although there have been very few confirmed cases of rabies in ferrets, when it does occur, it's always fatal. Many ferret owners don't believe this vaccine is necessary because their pets are never taken outdoors. However, ferrets are fantastic escape artists, and a runaway ferret could meet a rabid raccoon on his adventures.

There is only one approved rabies vaccine for ferrets in North America, and that is Imrab-3. Imrab-3 is what is known as a killed virus. This is important. If a mistake is made and a live virus vaccine is given to a ferret, he can actually come down with the disease. Be certain that your veterinarian gives the correct product. A kit should have a rabies immunization at the age of 12 weeks. An adult with a questionable vaccine history should have one immediately. Thereafter, all ferrets should be revaccinated yearly.

Here's another good reason for getting your ferret vaccinated against rabies—one that you might not have thought about. If your ferret nips or bites someone and that person either registers a complaint or seeks medical attention for the wound, there could be problems. Did you know that in many places, physicians are obligated to report animal bites to authorities? Although there has never been a documented case of rabies being transmitted from a ferret to a human, local animal control personnel in many jurisdictions have the power to seize your fuzzy, euthanize him, and have his brain examined for evidence of rabies. However, if your ferret is vaccinated, you might be able to persuade your local public health or animal control authority to follow the recently established protocol for ferrets that calls for quarantine rather than euthanasia after a biting incident.

Unfortunately, not all health departments know about or follow the protocol. Do you know what the policy is where you live? If not, you owe it to your fuzzy to find out the facts. Is your city, town, or county still in the dark ages? Does it still have a seize-and-destroy policy in effect for ferrets that nip or bite? If so, it's time to get hopping. Surf the Internet or contact ferret clubs to get your hands on the latest, most up-to-date information on this subject. Then lobby your local authorities to adopt the protocol that recommends quarantine rather than death row for ferrets that bite.

Don't wait for a problem to arise before you get down to the fact finding and the lobbying—it's too late then. If your ferret nips someone, he could be a goner before you can get mobilized. There have been dozens of tragic stories about cherished pets needlessly confiscated and euthanized for rabies testing. Don't let this happen to yours.

The rabies vaccination is not the only one your ferret needs. He also needs one for canine distemper. Ferrets are particularly susceptible to this disease. The distemper virus can be passed from an infected animal to another animal by direct contact such as licking or by indirect contact such as sneezing or coughing. However, your ferret doesn't need to be around an infected animal to come down with the disease—he can contract the virus just by walking over the urine or feces of an infected animal. In fact, you can even bring distemper home to your pet on the bottom of your shoes.

Distemper is virtually 100 percent fatal to ferrets; it is also a particularly distressing disease. The infected animal becomes very lethargic and anorexic, and he develops a thick discharge from the nose and eyes. His lips, chin, eyes, nose, and anus swell and become crusty; his paw pads become swollen, thick, and hard. An infected ferret keeps his eyes closed because they hurt. In the later stages of the illness, the brain is affected. At this point, hyperactivity, uncommon aggression, drooling, and seizures occur, followed by coma and death.

Who would willingly expose their favorite fuzzy to these miseries when a vaccine is readily available to prevent the disease? Fervac-D is the only USDA-licensed distemper vaccine labeled specifically for use with ferrets. However, some veterinarians use Galaxy-D, even though this vaccine is not specifically licensed for use in ferrets. Immunization against canine distemper involves a series of shots—the first is given at age 8 weeks, the next at 11 weeks, with the third inoculation at 14 weeks. Then, a yearly booster is necessary.

When buying a kit, ask what shots it has had. Ask, too, for proof of those shots. The little guy won't be fully protected against distemper unless he gets all three shots in the series. When purchasing an adult ferret with an unknown record of immunization, an immediate vaccination should be administered with a second shot three to four weeks later. Again, annual boosters are a must.

Because a small percentage of ferrets have allergic reactions to rabies and/or distemper vaccines, it is recommended that you wait with your pet in your veterinarian's office for at least 30 minutes after any inoculations just in case your pet has an adverse reaction. What are the signs of an allergic reaction? Your pet could experience stinging at the site of the injection. He could scream, vomit, have diarrhea or bloody diarrhea, act very hyper or very lethargic, get hives, or he could become cherry-red colored in the gums, ears, paw pads, and nose. He could also collapse suddenly and have trouble breathing (an anaphylactic reaction). All of these symptoms or just some of them may be

After your pet's immunization shots, stick around the veterinary clinic for 30 minutes just in case your furball has an allergic reaction.

present; the allergic reaction may be mild or severe. In rare instances, a ferret may have mild symptoms immediately following the shot and develop more severe symptoms several hours later. By waiting in your veterinarian's office, you can ensure that your pet gets prompt medical attention if necessary. Should your pet become ill after leaving the veterinary clinic, please return *immediately* because allergic reactions can be life threatening.

Many veterinarians inoculate ferrets against both rabies and distemper at the same office visit. If this is done and a reaction does occur, it's not possible to know which of the two vaccines is the culprit. For this reason, some ferret specialists now recommend that the two vaccines be given at least a few weeks apart.

Allergic reactions can happen at any age. A kit may have a reaction with its first injection. An older ferret may have one at age five or six or seven after having been vaccinated for years without a problem. There is no way to know in advance which ferrets will have a reaction or when a reaction will occur.

What do you do if your precious pet is one of the unlucky ferrets that has had a vaccine reaction? When yearly booster time comes around again, should he have the shot or not? This is always a difficult decision. On the one hand, your pet could have another adverse reaction to the vaccine, possibly even a life-threatening one. On the other hand, if he isn't vaccinated, he will most likely die if he contracts either rabies or distemper. An added complication is that, in some localities, ferret immunization is required. There is no easy answer to this dilemma. Your best bet is to discuss the whole question with your veterinarian.

Here are some points to consider. How serious was your ferret's reaction the last time? Is distemper or rabies prevalent in your area? Is your ferret more at risk from the vaccine or from the virus? Is another brand of vaccine a possibility? Your veterinarian might suggest giving your ferret an antihistamine injection before any future vaccinations to help ward off or minimize any reactions—this works in some cases but not in all. If you're really between a rock and a hard place—for example, your fuzzy has severe reactions to vaccines but there's an outbreak of distemper in your area—you could ask your vet about a blood test to determine whether your ferret's previous inoculations are still providing immunity. These titer tests are expensive, but they could be worth the expense if the results help you make an informed decision.

Foreign Bodies in the Digestive System

One of the most common reasons for ferrets to need medical attention is their tendency to ingest foreign objects. Ferrets have oddball tastes—they like to eat weird stuff like rubber, foam, latex, cloth, and sponge. Unfortunately, if your fuzzy snacks on any of these materials, he won't be able to digest them. He might be able to pass very small pieces in his poop, but larger bits can lodge in his stomach or get stuck in his intestines. Sometimes several small pieces bind together and cause the same problems as a large piece.

When a foreign body sits in the stomach, it can cause two problems. Bacteria can grow on the object itself, and/or the object can intermittently block the opening to the intestines. Symptoms to watch for are nausea (pawing at the mouth can be a sign of this), drooling, intermittent vomiting, loss of appetite, weight loss, tarry stools, thin ribbon-like stools, and depression.

Not only can the foreign object sit in the stomach, if the object is small enough it can pass through the stomach and into the intestinal tract. Because a ferret's intestinal tract is very narrow, it can easily be partially or totally blocked by an undigested object. If this happens, a ferret can have all of the above symptoms as well as a swollen abdomen, pain when defecating, and an absence of stools. A ferret with a blockage will look sick and act sick, often crying out in pain. This is a real emergency—death may occur within 24 to 48 hours without medical intervention. So, please, if any of these symptoms are present, seek *immediate* veterinary care for your pet. A foreign object that can't be passed needs to be surgically removed.

This holds true for hairballs, too. Like cats, ferrets lick themselves while grooming. Some of the licked hair sticks to their tongue and is swallowed. The hair then mats together in the stomach where it forms balls that continue to grow over time as more and more hair sticks to them. Unlike cats, ferrets can't cough up hairballs. A hairball, therefore, behaves like any other foreign object. It stays in the stomach or it passes into the intestinal tract and causes a blockage.

Fortunately, there is a lot you can do to prevent hairballs from becoming a problem. Prevention is the key here—take a twofold approach. First, brush your furball on a regular basis to get rid of loose hair that might otherwise be swallowed. Second, make cat or ferret hairball laxative part of your fuzzy's regular routine. A 0.5 to 1 inch (1.3 to 2.5 cm) long ribbon of this preventative medicine given two to three times per week will help any ingested hair to pass through the digestive tract. This is particularly important after baths and during the shedding periods that ferrets go through twice a year. But keep the tube well out of ferret reach. Most fuzzies love the stuff. In fact, some have been known to eat a whole tube of it—plastic and all!

Sponge, rubber, cork, and foam are just a few examples of what can get stuck in a ferret's digestive system.

Accidental Poisoning

Ferrets not only eat odd things, they also drink unusual things that other animals won't touch. Add to this the fact that ferrets can open cupboard doors, and it's obvious why they are susceptible to accidental poisoning. A ferret will lap up cleaning liquids like Pinesol and Lysol. He'll lick his lips over liquid

Don't forget to give your fuzzy regular doses of hairball laxative.

ant poison, plant fertilizers, car antifreeze, or toilet bowl cleaner. Prevention should be your first line of defense. Keep all cleaning solutions, caustic substances, and poisonous products out of reach or under lock and key.

However, if an accident should happen, don't delay. Rush your pet to the nearest veterinarian or emergency clinic for immediate treatment. You could also call the Animal Poison Control Center at 1-900-680-0000 to speak to a veterinarian who will advise you of what to do until you can get your pet to the vet. (There is a charge to your telephone bill for this service.)

One more point—never give your ferret any medication that has not been specifically recommended or prescribed for him by the vet or you may accidentally poison your pet yourself. What's safe for you or your family could kill your ferret.

Internal and External Parasites

Ferrets are susceptible to several different types of external and internal parasites. As a responsible owner, there are steps you can take to prevent many of these organisms from finding a home in or on your furball.

In many parts of North America, heartworm disease is a serious concern. Heartworm is a parasite that is carried by mosquitoes. It takes just one bite by an infected mosquito to transfer the parasite(s) to your pet. No problem, you might think—your fuzzy won't cross paths with a mosquito because he never goes outside. Think again. Have you got the only mosquito-proof house or apartment in North America? Remember, one insect bite is all it takes for the parasites to enter a ferret's bloodstream. Although they start out microscopic, these larvae soon grow into adult worms 5 inches (13 cm) long or more. Picture one or more of these in a ferret's small heart. It takes very few worms to prove fatal—in fact, even one can kill.

A ferret with heartworm disease will appear tired all the time, will be short of breath after mild exertion, and might have a cough—although other heart ailments can cause identical symptoms. Until recently, heartworm was an automatic death sentence for a ferret. But now, if the disease is diagnosed early enough, a new treatment protocol offers hope for survival. However, your ferret's best hope for survival is not to get the disease in the first place. If you live in a part of the country where heartworm is prevalent, ask your veterinarian for preventative medication for your fuzzy. Be sure to ask for the liquid form rather than the pill; it's much easier for a ferret to swallow, especially if mixed with Ferretone.

Be conscientious about giving the medication. It's important not to skip any dosages, to give it exactly as prescribed, and to use it for the whole mosquito season. Ferrets living in southern parts of the country will need the medication year-round.

Ear mites are other pesky pests that can bother your furball . . . they are quite common. These parasites, which are easily passed from one animal to another, cause irritation and inflammation in the ears. Most ferrets usually have *some* reddish brown ear wax, but excessive wax, wax with a black color, or wax that is smelly could indicate mites. If your ferret scratches his ears frequently, shakes his head a lot, or walks with a tilt, suspect ear mites. How can you be sure? Try shining a penlight into your ferret's ears—you might see signs of tiny white mite life. Or, get your veterinarian to do an ear swab.

Untreated ear mites can have serious health consequences for your pet, so you'll want to keep an eye on your ferret's ears and treat any mites promptly. Ear mite preparations made for cats are safe for ferrets, although a prescription from your veterinarian might be more

Just a little bit of Ferretone helps the medicine go down.

Keep house and ferret flea free.

potent. The medication goes directly into the ferret's ears. Be careful to follow directions exactly—if you don't, the mites might not be eliminated completely. Repeated treatments are necessary. In addition, take care of any stray mites on the fur by shampooing your ferret with a flea shampoo made for ferrets or cats. Pay particular attention to the tail. Why? Look at how your ferret sleeps—curled up in a ball, with his tail wrapped around his head. Those little mites can hop or crawl from ears to tail and back again.

Are there other pets in the house? Ear mites aren't picky about which animal ears they hop to and hang out in. Check the rest of your menagerie and treat any infected pets. Bedding and cage must be de-mited, too. Hot water, soap, and flea spray should do the trick.

Fleas and ticks are next on the list of bad bugs. There's nothing worse than a house full of fleas to get everyone scratching! Ferrets do

scratch a lot. It's not unusual for a fuzzy to stop in his tracks, scratch furiously, and then run on his way. But a ferret that scratches excessively could have fleas. Pick him up, separate his fur, and take a good look. Do you see any fast-moving, little black bodies? Or, how about droppings—tiny black specks of flea feces? Check between the shoulder blades, at the base of the tail, under the legs . . . these are favorite flea hangouts.

OK, you've seen the fleas, now how do you get rid of them? First, de-flea your ferret (and other pets, too). You'll find several ferret-specific flea shampoos on the pet shop shelves. Not many ferret products in your local pet shop? Then a flea shampoo made for kittens will do. Or, ask your veterinarian to recommend a product. Do not use flea shampoos made for dogs—and don't use flea collars, either.

A flea-free ferret won't stay that way for very long unless you de-flea the house, too. The biggest problem in flea control is not the fleas you see on your pet but the ones that you don't see crawling over carpets and bedding in your ferret's house and in your house, too. You'll have to go on the offensive and do battle with the fleas. Start with your ferret's house. Clean it out with hot water and soap, then spray it with a flea killer. Wash all the ferret's bedding in hot water. Empty and clean out the litter box(es). Next, attack your own house. Vacuum every square inch of every room, and throw out the vacuum bag. If the infestation is particularly heavy, use a flea and tick spray or bomb. Fleas are persistent little buggers. To wipe them out completely, you'll have to repeat the whole procedure several times until there are no traces of the pests.

What a hassle all this shampooing and house cleaning is! Why spend all the time, energy, and money exterminating fleas when you can prevent them instead with flea preventative medications like Advantage, Frontline Top Spot, and Program? These products, which work by disrupting the life cycle of the flea, will make your life a whole lot easier if you live in Flea Haven, USA. Depending on the product, you either rub it onto your pet or dole it out in some Ferretone once a month. Although these medications were developed for cats and dogs, they are widely used for ferrets, too. It's the cat formula that's given to ferrets; your veterinarian can recommend the correct dose for your particular pet.

In areas where ticks are common, be vigilant. After every walk, inspect your pet for these little blood suckers. Should you find a tick on your ferret, it's best to have your veterinarian remove it properly. When this isn't possible, you'll have to do it yourself. Remove the tick with tweezers, pulling firmly to dislodge it, head and all—heads not completely removed can become infected. Finally, destroy the varmint, and clean and disinfect the bite area.

Some ticks carry Lyme disease that can be transmitted to both you and your ferret. If Lyme disease is prevalent in your geographic area, take your ferret to a veterinarian as soon as possible after a tick bite—immediate treatment with antibiotics can make a difference in the disease's outcome.

The two most common internal parasites found in ferrets are Coccidia and *Giardia*. These microscopic, single-cell organisms live in an animal's intestinal tract and can be passed from one animal to another by contact with infected feces. A ferret can also contract *Giardia* by drinking from a contaminated outdoor water supply . . . don't allow your pet to drink from water puddles or ponds while walking outside. And if your ferret escapes from home, watch for symptoms of parasitic problems in case your runaway had a drink of fouled water while on the lam.

In ferrets, the two parasites prevent absorption of nutrients by the intestines. Symptoms are the same for both infections. They include soft stools, diarrhea or bloody diarrhea, loss of appetite, bloated tummy, dull coat, and/or general wasting. When either *Giardia* or Coccidia is suspected, your veterinarian will check your ferret's stools. Several samples over several days may be necessary because a single stool sample doesn't always test positive for parasites. Has your fuzzy been infected? Then your veterinarian will prescribe appropriate medication. Be sure to follow the directions carefully because the parasites are difficult to get rid of, especially in a multiple-ferret family. Be sure, too, to practice good hygiene because people can also become infected with *Giardia*.

Adrenal Disease

Adrenal disease is very common in ferrets three to four years old and older, although younger ferrets can also become stricken. The adrenal glands are located near the top of each kidney and produce hormones that are necessary for day-to-day functioning. In a ferret with adrenal disease, the hormones go into overdrive. This happens for a number of reasons. Sometimes a tumor or tumors (cancerous or not) grow in one or both glands. In other instances, the glands themselves become enlarged. In still other cases, the glands stay the same size but turn to a Jell-O-like substance and stop functioning properly.

Although a ferret doesn't always show any symptoms in the early stages of adrenal disease, after a while the signs become pretty obvious. The most common symptom is loss of hair. Baldness usually starts near the base of the tail and moves up the back and both sides of the body. Hair loss can be quite dramatic—a ferret can become almost bald in a short period of time. Repeated hair loss and regrowth is not unusual. The skin can become

Drinking from an outdoor water source can put your pet at risk of contracting parasites.

thin and *very* itchy; it can also become extremely dry and may develop scabs. Weight loss is common, and wasting causes a distinct sunken look to the lower-back area. Strange to say, even with wasting, a ferret can have a potbellied appearance because the disease causes fat to accumulate in the stomach area. Hormonal changes sometimes cause spayed females to have swelling of the vulva and a discharge—much the same as if they were coming into season. These same hormone changes can cause neutered males to become interested in mating activity. The body odor of both sexes may increase significantly. So may the incidence of urinary tract problems . . . watch for a ferret that runs to the litter box frequently but doesn't pass much urine.

Veterinarians can often diagnose adrenal gland problems just by looking at a ferret's symptoms. However, many veterinarians will want to do blood tests and perhaps ultrasound as well. The most common treatment is surgical removal of the affected gland or glands. In most cases, it's the left gland that's diseased. This is fortunate because it's the most easily removed. The right gland is much more difficult to remove because it's normally attached to the main blood vessel, the vena cava. So, when doing surgery on the right gland, veterinarians usually cut away what they can and leave the rest. However, innovative surgical

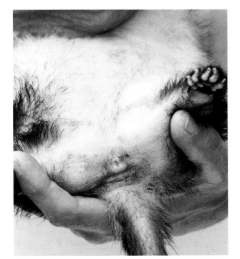

A swollen vulva in a spayed female is often an indication of adrenal disease.

techniques such as cryosurgery and microsurgery are now making it possible for the right gland to be removed completely and safely.

Although surgery is the treatment of choice for adrenal disease, sometimes a veterinarian may suggest drug therapy instead. For example,

Bear is going bald—a typical sign of adrenal disease. Notice, also, the hind-end wasting and the scabs on his skin where he has been scratching.

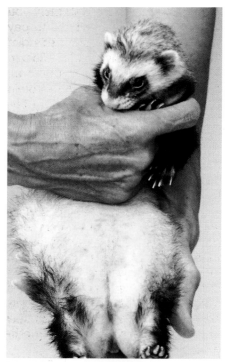

Another symptom of adrenal disease is a potbellied appearance.

• What kind of adrenal gland problem does the ferret have? Does he have tumors? Are they benign or malignant? Does he have enlargement of the gland(s)?
• How advanced is the disease at diagnosis?
• Does the ferret have any other medical problems?
• What type of treatment has been chosen?

After successful treatment, hair usually grows back, body odor returns to normal, a swollen vulva reduces to normal size, energy levels increase—in other words, the ferret gets back to being his/her old self again. However, there are no guarantees—results vary from ferret to ferret. Many live a few more years and have an excellent quality of life . . . others may get only a few extra months.

Insulinoma

Insulinoma is often, but not always, found in conjunction with adrenal disease. In North America, it is one of the most common ferret illnesses. Insulinomas are tumors of the pancreas. They produce excess insulin, and this in turn leads to low blood sugar (hypoglycemia) in the ferret. The tumors are most often the size of a pinhead but can be larger or smaller. There can be a single tumor or multiple tumors. There can also be cloud insulinomas, which are invisible, microscopic tumors dispersed throughout the pancreas.

old or sick ferrets may not be good candidates for surgery. If neither surgery nor drug treatment is an option (usually due to financial considerations), ask your veterinarian how you can make your pet's life as comfortable as possible for the months or years he has left. Using an antihistamine like Benadryl to control itching, slathering on a good-quality lotion to alleviate dry skin, and providing soft, warm bedding for your bald buddy can go a long way to improving his quality of life.

The outcome of adrenal disease depends on a number of factors:

Unfortunately, insulinomas can be growing in a ferret well before any symptoms appear. However, eventually low blood sugar levels will lead to symptoms such as sluggishness, nausea (which causes a ferret to paw at its mouth), depression, drooling, and staggering. A ferret may even stop or drop in his tracks and stare blankly into space. He may sleep more frequently or for longer periods, and he may be very difficult to wake up. In advanced stages of the disease, semiconsciousness and seizures sometimes occur. It's important to know that the signs of the disease can come and go as blood sugar levels go up and down.

When a ferret is suffering any of these symptoms, blood tests should be done to determine if he has low blood sugar levels (glucose levels). Other tests may be recommended as well. When insulinoma is diagnosed, treatment can lengthen a ferret's life and improve the quality of life. Whether the treatment of choice involves surgery and/or drugs depends on many variables. If you're thinking about surgery, realize that the tumors often recur, so your ferret may be facing several surgeries. If you're thinking about medication, realize that medication levels will need to be increased as time goes on and the disease progresses. Medication treats only the symptoms, it doesn't cure the disease. Each ferret should have a treatment program based on his individual needs, so your best plan is to discuss the whole issue with your veterinarian.

Regardless of what treatment you opt for, you'll definitely have to pay special attention to your ferret's diet when he has insulinoma. In addition to his regular high-protein dry food, give him several small, high-protein meals every day. You could try tidbits of cooked meat and chicken or spoonfuls of turkey, lamb, and veal baby food (it helps to warm it up a bit). Or, tempt your fuzzy with a special high-protein canned a/d cat food that's available from your vet.

Nix all sweet treats and sugary supplements. Although sweets temporarily raise blood sugar levels, these higher glucose levels cause more insulin to be produced, which in turn lowers the blood sugar levels again. You should also ask your veterinarian if furball medicine can stay on the menu—most furball medicines have a sugar base.

Unfortunately, most insulinomas are eventually fatal, either because of hypoglycemia-induced complications or because the tumors spread to other organs. You do what you can to make your furball's quality of life as good as possible for as long as possible.

Lymphosarcoma

Lymphosarcoma is cancer of the lymph nodes and other organs of the lymph system like the liver and spleen—all of these are part of a ferret's immune system. This disease can occur in either sex at any age. The most telltale sign is enlarged lymph nodes, usually around the neck, under the rear and/or front legs, behind the knees, and in the thighs. These nodes may feel enlarged and hard like marbles. There may be internal tumors as well. Other symptoms to look for include an enlarged spleen (but this is common in ferrets for a variety of reasons), labored breathing, panting, tiredness, lack of appetite, wasting, stool changes, hind-end weakness, and fever. Many ferrets have no symptoms at all for months or years, so the disease is often far advanced before it's diagnosed.

Diagnosis is usually by blood tests and a biopsy of the lymph nodes. The disease is most often fatal in young ferrets because the cancer spreads quickly in growing young-

Lymphosarcoma is a cancer of the immune system.

sters. In older ferrets, lymphosarcoma usually progresses more slowly and survival seems to be longer with treatment. Chemotherapy is the recommended treatment, and most ferrets tolerate it quite well. However, not every owner can afford chemotherapy for a pet.

Skin Tumors

Skin tumors usually present themselves as lumps under the skin or on the surface of the skin. Some tumors look like red, raised scabs, others may be crusty and rough, still others look like warts. Whenever you bathe your ferret, check his skin for any abnormalities. This is especially important for ferrets over three years of age. If you find anything on your pet's skin that looks out of the ordinary, don't sit around waiting to see if it goes away—make an appointment with your veterinarian right away.

The best treatment for a skin tumor, whether benign or malignant, is surgical removal. In the case of malignant tumors, prompt removal prevents their spread. Your vet will probably recommend that a piece of the tumor be sent to a laboratory for analysis so you both know what you're dealing with.

Chondromas are tumors that sometimes grow on the tip of an older ferret's tail. Although benign, these can grow very large and sore, so they need to be surgically removed.

ECE

Epizootic catarrhal enteritis is the dreaded ECE, a *highly* contagious viral illness also known as green slime disease. The virus attacks the lining of a ferret's intestinal tract, damaging the intestinal membranes. Although it's not often fatal if appropriate nursing care is given, this disease can be a ferret owner's nightmare.

Some ferrets seem to be more affected by ECE than others. For example, kits don't often get sick from the virus, and when they do, the symptoms are minimal. They can, however, be carriers. The same holds true for ferrets six years old and older. The hardest hit are ferrets between the ages of two years and four years old. In this group, the severity of the illness ranges from very mild to very severe.

ECE can be spread directly from ferret to ferret, or it can be spread unwittingly when an owner handles an infected ferret and then handles his or her own—the virus hitches a ride home on clothing or skin. Cases have even been reported where neither owners nor their ferrets had any exposure at all to other ferrets—so even a totally isolated ferret is not completely safe from the virus.

Protecting your ferret against the disease is more of a problem than you might think. Some ferrets that are not showing signs of the illness can be carriers of the disease. Other ferrets that have recovered from the virus can still be contagious for months or even a year after recuperation. So you have no way of knowing whether or not a ferret you are handling is carrying the virus. You could pick up the virus from that cute little kit you're cuddling at the pet shop and carry it home to your ferret. Your fuzzy could bring home more than a blue ribbon from Ferret Fun Day. A new addition to your ferret household could come toting more than his sleep sack. Before you or your ferret have contact with other ferrets, weigh up the situation carefully—it's up to you to protect your pet.

After being exposed to the ECE virus, a ferret takes between 24 and 72 hours to show symptoms. Usually, vomiting and lethargy are the first symptoms. However, you might not notice your ferret has thrown up if he has free run of the house and vomits under a chair. You might not even notice that your furball has become lethargic and uninterested in food. But you'll certainly notice (or smell) the green diarrhea that comes along next—ECE isn't called green slime disease for nothing. Although green diarrhea can be a sign of other health problems, the diarrhea that goes along with ECE is unmistakable. It's explosive, watery, foul smelling, and ranges in color from a dark forest green to a bright, almost fluorescent green. It may also be accompanied by what looks like long, white worms. These white stringy things are not worms—they are pieces of the intestinal tract lining being shed.

This green diarrhea usually lasts for two to four days. If it's profuse and frequent, get your pet to the vet right away. Prolonged diarrhea can lead to dehydration, and dehydration can be fatal for ferrets. To ensure your pet's survival, your veterinarian may need to give it subcutaneous (injected under the skin) or intravenous fluids.

Most owners think that the disease has run its course as soon as the green poops stop. But don't be fooled. It's just when you're congratulating yourself that the crisis is over that the worst phase of the disease hits. What happens is that your ferret loses all interest in food. This is a very serious situation. When ferrets don't eat, stomach acids attack the mucous membranes of their digestive tracts, and they quickly develop ulcers of the mouth, esophagus, and stomach. These ulcers are so painful that your pet won't want to eat . . . and so starts the cycle. When your pet is sick, he has no appetite. When he doesn't eat, ulcers develop. When the ulcers hurt, he doesn't eat. When he doesn't eat, the ulcers get worse. Get the picture?

So what can you do? You must watch your ferret's food intake carefully as soon as the green diarrhea starts and even more carefully when it stops. Not only is it important to monitor daytime eating, it's important to monitor nighttime intake, too—count the pieces of dry food in his bowl before bedtime and again in the morning. A ferret should eat a minimum of 20 pieces of food between bedtime and breakfast. He's not? Then he's not getting enough nourishment.

If your pet refuses to eat, you must take steps to make sure that he does. Otherwise, he could die. To encourage an appetite, moisten his regular dry food with warm water to make it more palatable. You might try holding single pieces of wetted food between your fingertips, on the palm of your hand, or on a plastic spoon. A sick ferret that's not interested in food will sometimes eat if he's hand-fed. Your ferret still won't take a bite? Try adding enough water to the food to make a soft mush. Microwave the mush to warm it slightly, then hand-feed your fuzzy.

No luck yet? Prepare one of the special food recipes in the "Grub and Gruel for Sick Ferrets" section on page 159, and hand-feed it to your pet. Because these recipes are laced with goodies, your furball may lap up this special grub even though he's turning up his nose at everything else. A note of warning here . . . if your ferret is suffering from other health problems, especially insulinoma, please talk to your veterinarian before using any of the gruel recipes. The sugar content in some of them may be too high for a ferret with insulinoma.

Ferrets that stop eating often stop drinking as well. If your sick ferret won't drink from a sipper bottle or bowl, dip your fingers into water and encourage him to lick them. Dip-lick, dip-lick, dip-lick is the best way to keep your ferret drinking. Be sure to offer water or, better yet, Pedialyte, at every feeding and between feedings. Pedialyte is a liquid that replaces necessary salts, sugars, and minerals that are lost when a pet has excessive diarrhea or vomiting. Look for it, or other electrolyte replacement products, in the baby section of the pharmacy or grocery store.

A ferret that won't eat and drink on his own or when hand-fed must be force-fed as a last resort. Many owners cringe at the thought. But you have to put your fuzzy's well-being ahead of your squeamish stomach. Force-feeding is not pleasant for either pet or owner, but it's sometimes necessary to save a pet's life.

Your invalid's not going to like being force-fed—though sick, he'll struggle like crazy. So, you'll have to truss him up. Take a cutoff sweatpant leg or a hockey sock, and pop your ferret into it so that only his head is sticking out. Wind a long shoelace round and round your pet to wrap him up. The trick is to bundle him tightly enough so he can't wiggle loose but not so tightly that he's uncomfortable (see photo). Now, truss yourself up in towels or an apron to protect your clothes from spewed, spit, or splattered food. Then lay your reluctant patient on your lap or clamp him under one arm.

Using a needleless syringe from the vet or the drugstore, draw up 5 cc to 10 cc of warmed gruel mix (see end of chapter). The recipe must be thin enough to be sucked up into the syringe and squirted out again a

Trussing your pet makes force-feeding easier.

drop at a time. If it's not, add more Pedialyte or water. Put the syringe to your ferret's lips, and squirt a tiny amount into his mouth. He should soon start licking at the food. Keep it coming in little squirts, making sure you give him time to swallow—30 cc to 60 cc is what you're aiming to get into him at a sitting.

For that stubborn pain in the neck that shakes his head and clamps down those jaws at mealtimes, insert the tip of the syringe at the side of his mouth, right at the back teeth. Squeeze a few drops into his mouth, and watch carefully to see that he swallows them. Some ferrets bite on the syringe when it's inserted at the back of the mouth. This is OK, as long as you slowly squirt a few drops as he's biting. Alternate a syringe of food with a few cc's of water or Pedialyte. Take things *very* slowly, and be extremely careful that your ferret doesn't choke on the forced food or water. At every feeding, offer a few pieces of moistened regular food because your goal is to encourage a return to normal eating patterns as soon as possible.

Because ECE leads to the loss or damage of the intestinal lining, a ferret isn't able to absorb as many nutrients from his food as usual. In fact, when the diarrhea stops, you'll notice his stools will take on a birdseed appearance. The seeds are tiny bits of food that can't be digested by the damaged intestines. When your ferret's intestines aren't working properly, you have to take charge so he won't waste away. Not only do you have to feed him highly nutritious food, you have to make sure that he gets it at regular intervals. Try to feed a sick ferret at least every four hours around the clock. If you work or go to school, you might have to enlist the help of a relative or a friend, dash home on your lunch hour, take personal leave or vacation time, hire a pet sitter for feedings, get help from a local ferret club, take your ferret to work, beg for flex time, or go a little longer between feedings. Only you know what kind of arrangements you can make. Base your decisions on how ill your ferret is—you might even have to have him hospitalized to get him through the crisis period.

Force-feeding may be necessary for only a few days, but in severe cases, you might have to continue for a few weeks or even a couple of months. Your ferret may even eat normally for a day or two and then stop eating again. So keep monitoring his food and water intake until eating habits return to normal.

When you realize how many medical problems can stem from ECE—vomiting, diarrhea, dehydration, anorexia, ulcers, secondary infections—then you'll realize that you should have a veterinarian's input from the onset of the disease. Your vet can advise you about both over-the-counter and prescription medication that may be necessary to control diarrhea, coat the stomach, control stomach acid, treat the ulcers, control nausea and vomiting, increase appetite, and ward off secondary infections. Your veterinarian can also instruct you on force-feeding if it's necessary. As well as getting invaluable medical advice from your veterinarian, you can also get information and support from ferret clubs and from ferret web sites.

ECE need not be fatal. In fact, if proper nursing care is given, very few ferrets die from the disease. Those that do usually have some other underlying illness that had weakened their systems before ECE struck. The good news is that the majority of ferrets that have had the virus and recover don't get it again.

But please kept in mind that ferrets that have had the disease can be carriers of the virus for up to ten months or longer. So, if your furball has had ECE, you have a big responsibility to make sure that neither your fuzzy nor you pass it on to other ferrets. *Don't handle ferrets of any age at pet stores, shelters, or friends' houses.* And don't take your fuzzy or yourself to a fair, a show, or any other ferret get-together for at least a year after your pet has recovered.

Unfortunately, there is no vaccine to protect ferrets against the ECE virus. However, the specific virus has now been identified, which opens the door to further research and possible vaccine development. If the happy day does come when a vaccine is available, don't delay—get that fuzzy vaccinated ASAP.

Aleutian Disease

Aleutian disease (ADV) is another virus that affects ferrets. Fortunately, it's not very common in North America, and most ferrets that test positive for Aleutian disease will never become sick with it. For the small percentage of ferrets that do develop an active case of ADV, the symptoms are progressive weight loss, wasting, enlarged liver and/or spleen, hind-leg weakness, staggering, and tarry stools. In some instances, the virus causes sudden death with no prior symptoms.

Aleutian disease can be spread through the air or by direct ferret-to-ferret contact. It can also be spread by contact with contaminated saliva, urine, or feces. In fact, the virus is so

hardy it can hang around for over two years on surfaces that haven't been properly disinfected. You, yourself, can spread ADV, too. You can take it home on your hands or clothing after handling an infected ferret.

There is no vaccine, no treatment, and no cure for ADV. Most ferrets that develop an active form of the virus will die. For this reason, it's very important to prevent the spread of the disease. If you have an ADV-positive ferret—even one that's symptom free—keep yourself and your pet well away from ferret get-togethers, from other ferret owners, and from pet stores that sell ferrets.

Aplastic Anemia

Aplastic anemia happens when a female ferret is in heat (or in season) for a prolonged period of time. When

A sick ferret should be examined and evaluated by a veterinarian.

a jill goes into heat, her body produces high levels of the hormone estrogen. The estrogen levels stay high until she becomes pregnant, has a false pregnancy by being mated with a vasectomized male, or receives a hormone injection. If none of these things happen, the jill continues in heat, and hormone levels remain high. Excess estrogen can prevent the bone marrow from producing enough red blood cells, white blood cells, and platelets (blood-clotting agents). A decrease in blood cells leads to life-threatening anemia and infections. A decrease in platelets can cause internal bleeding.

Unspayed, unbred females have a high chance of developing aplastic anemia. Symptoms include lack of appetite, hair loss (patchy to total baldness), listlessness, depression, pale gums and nose, and hind-end weakness. In advanced stages of the condition, there can be a foul-smelling discharge from the vulva. Unfortunately, symptoms may not always be apparent until a jill is very sick.

Treatment can sometimes be effective in the early stages of aplastic anemia. When the condition is diagnosed soon enough, spaying can save a jill's life. In some cases, blood transfusions, medications, vitamin therapy, intravenous fluids, and force-feeding may also be required. If aplastic anemia develops beyond the early stages, however, damage to the bone marrow is usually so severe that treatment can't reverse it and the jill dies.

The best way to deal with aplastic anemia is to prevent it. Spay that female ferret if she's not to be used for breeding.

Respiratory Problems

Ferrets are one of the few pets that can catch a cold or the flu virus from people. Anyone who has a cold or the sniffles should not handle, sneeze on, or cough around the family ferret. What do you do, then, when you have a cold but your fuzzy needs care and attention? Your best bet is to hand over ferret chores to a cold-free family member. That's not possible? Then wash your hands often and carefully with soap and hot water, especially before handling or feeding time. As an added protection, wear a face mask so your germs are less likely to become your ferret's germs.

A ferret with a cold could sneeze, cough a bit, have a runny nose and watery eyes, lack energy, and be uninterested in food. Think how you feel when you have a cold and a stuffed-up nose—your ferret feels the same way. Extra rest and a little petroleum jelly around the nose to prevent caking can help a lot. A room humidifier can make breathing easier, though a really stuffy nose might need some vet-recommended medication. *Never* give your ferret aspirin without the express direction of a veterinarian . . . owner-prescribed dosages have been known to cause ferret deaths.

Is your ferret totally listless? Does he have a yellow or green nasal discharge? Is he having difficulty breathing, rapid breathing, or rattling noises when breathing? Contact your veterinarian immediately. Pneumonia could be developing, or the respiratory problems could be a sign of other serious illness.

Heart Disease

The most common heart problem in ferrets is cardiomyopathy, or disease of the heart muscle. It occurs most frequently in ferrets three years of age or older. A ferret with heart disease will be tired and sleep a lot; he'll lack energy and often flop down after minimal exertion. He'll probably have shortness of breath and maybe some coughing. A veterinarian checking your ferret may find a faster-than-normal heartbeat and possible pulse irregularities. In advanced stages of the disease, a ferret with cardiomyopathy will have bluish-colored gums, swollen legs and feet, and labored breathing.

X rays, ultrasound, and electrocardiograms are used to diagnose heart disease in ferrets. Medication can often control, but not cure, heart disease. It's important to give all medication according to your veterinarian's instructions. It's also important to make sure your ferret sticks to any diet restrictions ordered by your veterinarian. And don't push your ferret to take part in all of the activities he used to enjoy—a fuzzy with heart disease needs to rest a lot. Let your ferret be the judge. When he wants to play—play. When he's had enough, curl up on the sofa together.

Urinary Tract Problems and Prolapsed Rectum

Ferrets, both male and female, can develop urinary tract troubles. Bladder infections and bladder stones show up in both sexes, while prostate dysfunction can be an additional problem for males. A ferret that's having difficulty passing urine may run in and out of his litter box often, either because he's passing

Your fuzzy can catch your cold—take precautions when playing with him.

small amounts of urine frequently or because he has the urge to urinate but can't. When a blockage is the culprit, a ferret may even cry out in pain when trying to urinate. If you notice that your pet is making more trips than usual to the litter box, if he's crying in the litter box, if he has blood in his urine or blood staining the fur around the urethra, then it's time for a trip to the vet.

When a small section of intestine is pushed out through the anus, this is known as a prolapsed rectum. If your ferret has this problem, you'll notice a small, pink, tubular projection sticking out from his anus. It may or may not be present all of the time. Often it appears after a bowel movement, especially if the ferret has diarrhea or constipation and is straining to relieve himself. Usually the prolapse retracts into the anus shortly after a bowel movement, but in more severe cases, it can protrude more often than not. Because the moist, protruding tissue can be scraped and cut or can pick up litter and bacteria, infection is a concern. A ferret with a prolapsed rectum should always be checked over by a veterinarian.

There is some question as to whether early descenting predisposes a ferret to prolapsed rectum problems. There is also the possibility that kits fed dry food right after weaning may get a prolapsed rectum from straining to pass the harder stools. It's a good idea to moisten a kit's dry food with water for the first few weeks.

Back Injuries

With their long, slinky bodies and their love of climbing and jumping,

Heart disease will slow a ferret down.

ferrets are more susceptible than most pets to back sprains, strains, and injuries. A leap from the sofa, a free fall from the bookcase, or a tumble from a hammock can lead to muscle strain or worse. And, ferrets are so quick and so quiet that they can easily get underfoot and stepped on—not the best thing for an animal that's mostly back! If your ferret is limping, wincing when he walks, or not moving around as much as usual, consult the veterinarian.

In many cases, however, what you think is a back problem may not be a spinal injury at all. Hind-end paralysis, where the ferret loses the use of his hind legs, is a case in point. Although this is sometimes due to a back problem, it's more often an indication of a systemic disease or disorder such as adrenal cancer, aplastic anemia, cardiomyopathy, insulinoma, or lymphosarcoma.

Hair Loss

The two main reasons for generalized hair loss and baldness in a ferret are adrenal gland disease and aplastic anemia; cancer of the reproductive system can also be a cause. Other conditions can lead to localized hair loss. For example, a ferret could have patchy hair loss if suffering from mast cell tumors of the skin.

Sometimes, even when your pet's coat and skin are looking just fine, his tail can lose hair and get a scrawny, ratty look to it. This is most likely a condition called tail alopecia, a.k.a. stud tail or rat tail. The signs of tail alopecia are bald spots on a ferret's tail or a totally bald tail—with or without coarse tufts of hair, reddish brown waxy areas, and blackheads. When rat tail is the problem, you won't see hair loss anywhere else on the body. The good thing is that the hair usually grows back and your ferret will look like new again. Tail alopecia may happen only once in a ferret's life, or it can happen repeatedly. Veterinarians don't know what causes this condition, but hair loss on only the tail is not usually a cause for concern.

Does your fuzzy have a bald spot from being shaved for surgery? Don't be surprised if the hair takes a while to grow back. Also, in darker ferrets, when the hair begins to grow in, the skin frequently has a bluish or olive cast to it. Although this looks like bruising, it isn't. The discoloration is caused by the new hair follicles getting near the surface of the skin.

Heatstroke

Would you wear a fur coat on a hot day? Of course not! Unfortunately, your ferret has no choice. Wrapped in fur from head to toe, he has difficulty coping when the mercury climbs to 80°F (27°C). And when the temperature hits 90°F (32°C), he could die. Ferrets can't sweat, so they have no way of releasing excess body heat. This makes them particularly prone to heatstroke. Many owners have had a very sick ferret on their hands before they realized that their pet was suffering from the heat.

Symptoms of heatstroke include panting, listlessness, lethargy, drooling, and bright-red paw pads and nose. In severe cases, collapse and seizures occur. If you suspect that your ferret is suffering from the heat, take immediate steps to lower his body temperature. Place him belly down onto a cool surface, such as a concrete floor. Use washcloths soaked in cool, not cold, water, and apply them to the ferret's back, head, paws, legs, and tail. A quicker way to cool your ferret off is to lower him into a sink full of cool water, but this might be a bit traumatic, especially for ferrets that don't like baths.

This is what rat tail or stud tail looks like.

Do you live in an area where the summers are very hot? Then you'll have to take special precautions if you want to have a ferret as a pet. Ferrets cannot tolerate hot houses. Will fans keep your ferret cool? Not when the weather's really hot—they just blow hot air around. Air-conditioning is the only way to go when the mercury soars. But be sure to have a backup plan, too, in case of a power outage. Think friend's house, vet's office, air-conditioned car—anywhere that will keep your fuzzy cool and you calm.

Don't take a ferret outside in the summer heat, keep him out of hot cars, and make sure his cage is kept out of direct sunlight. It is *very* important to monitor the temperature in your ferret's environment. Remember, heat can kill.

Eye Ailments

Ferrets can suffer from a variety of eye ailments. Diminished vision, for example, sometimes occurs as a ferret becomes elderly. The old eyes just don't see as well as they used to.

Impaired vision can also be caused by cataracts. This disorder causes the lens of the eye to cloud over. Although some cataracts can be detected only by medical examination, in most cases they are visible and look like a milky white disk in the eye. Cataracts can affect the eyes of both young and old ferrets. In youngsters, they're usually hereditary, though they can be caused by an injury. In older ferrets, they're usually due to aging, though again, they can be the result of injury. Cataracts usually develop slowly, causing progressive loss of vision and eventual blindness. There is no treatment, but there's a lot you can do to help your ferret adjust to life with limited vision. See page 130 for training tips.

Inflammation and abnormal discharge are other eye ailments to watch for. They can crop up for a number of reasons—colds, infections, blocked tear ducts, foreign objects, allergies, and injuries. Don't mess with the eyes. Anything unusual eye-wise and it's time for a visit to the veterinarian.

Dental Problems

Although ferrets are born toothless, they get their 30 baby teeth within two to three weeks of birth. The 34 permanent teeth are in and working by the time they're ten weeks old.

Dental hygiene involves more than just cleaning teeth. It also involves checking your ferret's mouth regularly. Does your furball have any loose or broken teeth, tooth discolorations, or bad breath? Are his gums swollen, red, or bleeding? Does his mouth seem sensitive? Is he having difficulty eating? Anything unusual should be brought to the attention of your veterinarian. Your ferret can't announce that he has a toothache—it's up to you to watch for the signs.

Was your fuzzy born with crooked or protruding teeth? Be extra observant. Crooked teeth can trap food, and protruding teeth can cause mouth sores where they press on skin or gums. Oddly angled teeth may have to be extracted by a veterinarian.

A ferret's yearly health checkup should include a dental exam. Heavy buildup of tartar and plaque calls for professional teeth cleaning, and this has to be done under general anesthetic. Any tartar and plaque not removed can lead to swollen and bleeding gums, loose teeth, and tooth loss. Feeding your ferret a dry-food diet can help keep those chompers in tip-top shape.

One last word on tooth care— NEVER, NEVER, NEVER break off or trim your pet's canine teeth. Unfortunately, these ferret fangs are sometimes removed, broken off, or filed down by owners who mistakenly think that doing so will stop a ferret from biting. It won't. Teeth should be removed or trimmed only by a veterinarian and only if there is a *medical* reason to do so (for example, when a tooth is growing at an odd angle).

Grub and Gruel for Sick Ferrets

When sick, ferrets often lose their appetite. This can have serious consequences. Remember, ferrets eat approximately every four hours and

A cataract looks like a white, milky disk in the center of the eye.

digest their food quickly. So when they stop eating, they can go downhill rapidly. This is where you come in—you have to ensure that your ferret gets nourishment even when he's turning up his nose at his favorite ferret kibble. Tempt him with the following recipes. (Note: If your ferret suffers from insulinoma, check with your veterinarian before serving up any of these gruels—sugar content may be too high in some.)

The a/d solution
• 1 can (5.5 oz or 170 g) of Hill's Science Diet a/d canned food (available by prescription from veterinarians)
• Pedialyte (optional) or water

a/d canned food can be fed straight from the can or mixed with Pedialyte or water. You can make it as soupy as you need to, depending on whether your pet is lapping it from a spoon or being fed from a syringe. Most ferrets prefer it warmed up a bit in the microwave.

Veterinarians often recommend Science Diet a/d as the food of choice for sick ferrets and for force-feeding. Because it's packed with calories and protein and because it's highly digestible, this food packs more punch per mouthful than home-made mixes. The leftovers can be kept covered in the refrigerator for 24 hours or frozen in ice cube trays and then stored in airtight containers.

Patch's Pabulum
• ½ cup (120 mL) of dry ferret food
• ¼ cup (50 mL) of Pedialyte (or water)
• ½ cup (120 mL) of Ensure or Sustical (strawberry or vanilla, but no chocolate, please)
• 1 tablespoon (15 mL) of fatty acid supplement (such as Ferretone, Furotone, or similar)

Grind up the dry ferret food in a coffee bean grinder, food chopper, or food processor until it's the consistency of coffee grounds. Mix in the Pedialyte, the Ensure, and the fatty acid supplement. The mixture will look like thick soup. Ferrets like this pabulum warm, so pop it into the microwave for 20 seconds or until it's at body temperature. Stir well to ensure there are no hot spots (test with your finger), then offer it to your ferret on a plastic spoon. Gruel that sits too long will thicken—add more liquid as required. For force-feeding, make the mixture thin enough that it can be sucked up into a syringe. If you have several ferrets to feed, rewarm the pabulum as necessary.

Leftover mixture can be kept in the refrigerator for up to 24 hours. After that, it must be frozen in ice cube trays. Put 2 tablespoonfuls, or 30 cc, into each cube, and plan on feeding one to two cubes per ferret per meal.

Janie's Slop
• 1 cup (240 mL) of your pet's favorite dry ferret food
• 1 cup (240 mL) of his regular drinking water
• 1 can (5.5 oz or 170 g) of Hill's Science Diet a/d canned food
• 1 small jar of chicken baby food
• 1 small jar of chicken-and-rice baby food
• capsules of Tahitian noni (from the health-food store)

Soak the dry food in the water until mushy. Add all the rest of the ingredients except the noni capsules and mix well. If the slop is too thick, stir in extra water. Microwave till warm. At one mealtime each day, stir in the powder from one capsule of Tahitian noni. Freeze any leftover mixture in ice cube trays, and store in airtight containers.

All of the above recipes are good for feeding sick ferrets. Don't be upset, though, if your patient doesn't dive right in. He may have to get used to the taste first. Put a little food onto your finger, and dab it onto his upper lip beneath his nose.

That little tongue will soon take a taste. Be patient. Sick ferrets usually need encouragement. A ferret that refuses to eat a full meal—1 to 2 ounces, or 30 cc to 60 cc, or 2 to 4 tablespoons—should be fed smaller meals more frequently. A fuzzy that downright refuses food may need to be force-fed to survive—see page 151. (Note: never force-feed your pet if you suspect that he has an intestinal blockage.)

Although there's a lot you can do to help your sick pet—like nursing, meal preparation, and hand-feeding—never forget that an ill ferret should be examined and evaluated by a ferret-knowledgeable veterinarian. A sick furball has the best chance of survival when you and your vet work hand in hand to pull him through.

Where's the grub?

Chapter Sixteen

Reproduction and Breeding

A Brief Overview

For most ferret owners, breeding their pets is not something they have to concern themselves with because the majority of pet ferrets in the United States and Canada are already spayed and neutered when purchased. Fixed ferrets make the best house pets because they don't have that skunky smell or greasy fur, they're less likely to urine mark, and they're less aggressive.

Although there is some controversy about *when* to fix ferrets—at six weeks or at six months—there's no controversy about the fact that they should be fixed. There are too many ferrets sitting in shelters waiting for good homes as it is. It would be irresponsible to add to this problem.

The information on reproduction and breeding provided in this chapter is not meant to encourage owners to breed their ferrets. It's simply given as a brief overview to round out ferret owners' knowledge about their pets.

Photoperiodism

The reproductive cycle of ferrets is tied to the hours of light in the day. Ferrets are photoperiodic breeders. This means that the number of hours of daylight per day—or possibly the number of hours of darkness per night—determines when they come into season or heat and when the reproductive period ends.

In natural lighting conditions, neither male nor female ferrets are in season year-round. They can be bred only through the spring and summer. However, some breeders can manipulate lighting conditions so that ferrets are no longer confined to their natural breeding season but are able to produce litters at any time of the year.

Males

The male ferret's reproductive cycle is triggered when the days start to get longer, usually around the beginning of the year. At this time, his testicles start to drop into the scrotum. Over the next couple of months, the testes slowly enlarge so that they're fully developed and the hob's ready for action before the female comes into heat. He maintains his ability to breed until late summer, at which point his testes start to get smaller and eventually retract up into his body.

When a hob is in a state of sexual readiness, he stinks. Not only is his body odor very strong, the smell of his urine gets stronger, too. If he hasn't been doing so already, he'll start marking his territory with urine. Worse yet, to increase his sex appeal, he'll even dab himself with Eau de Urine. Skin and fur get very greasy—so much so that an albino's fur will take on a marked yellow cast.

Females

The female ferret's reproductive cycle is triggered by her pituitary gland when there is an average of 14 hours of uninterrupted daylight per day. At this point, usually in early spring, the female comes into heat, also known as estrus. It's very obvious when she does—her vulva swells to many times its normal size and becomes pink and protruding. In addition, there may be a watery discharge. Jills in heat also have a stronger, muskier body odor and greasier skin.

Female ferrets are induced ovulators. This means that even though they are in heat, they won't release eggs for fertilization until mating

takes place. If mating doesn't take place, ovulation won't occur, and the jill will stay in heat for the whole length of the breeding season. This condition is called prolonged estrus, and it can be very dangerous for a jill. Her exposed vulva makes her susceptible to infections. The production of the hormone estrogen over a long period of time can lead to a serious medical condition known as aplastic anemia (see Chapter 15). Many female ferrets die from the complications associated with prolonged estrus.

The only practical way to avoid the health problems that go along with prolonged estrus is to have your jill spayed before she comes into heat for the first time. Breeders

Spayed and neutered ferrets make good house pets.

This jill is caring for her newborn kits.

hob often bites the jill's neck, causing wounds and bleeding or, at the very least, a sore neck. For owners of house pets, the whole experience can be alarming and upsetting.

Birthing and Litters

After mating is successful, the gestation period is 42 days. Complications don't usually arise during the birth itself, but if they do, medical care will be needed immediately or the jill and/or kits can die. Litter size varies—on the low end there could be one bouncing baby; on the high end there could be 17 bundles of joy. However, the average litter size is more likely to be eight. At birth, each kit weighs less than 0.33 ounces (8 to 10 g), and its eyes and ears are sealed shut. Its skin is pink and covered with soft, white, downy fuzz. For the first three weeks, kits depend completely on their mother's milk. At three weeks of age, they start to eat some solid food but continue to nurse until they are weaned at about six weeks of age.

sometimes give their jills hormone injections (a.k.a. the jill jab) to end estrus, or they use a vasectomized hob to bring on a false pregnancy, but these options aren't too practical for your house pet. After all, how many vasectomized male ferrets are living on your street?

After birth, some jills have problems with insufficient milk production or with mastitis (inflammation of the mammary glands). Unless a foster mother can be found to nurse the kits, they will starve. Some Good Samaritans might attempt hand-feeding . . . but hand-feeding newborns is a huge undertaking. The kits have to be fed every two hours right around the clock, and the success rate is not high.

Mating

The best time for mating to take place is when the male's testes are fully developed and the female's vulva is fully enlarged. Don't expect a courteous courtship—the mating itself is noisy and violent. The male chases the jill, grabs her by the scruff of the neck, and drags her around. The jill in turn does a lot of squealing when she's attacked. The

Leave It to the Experts

Few ferrets in North America are kept outdoors. Most of them live under the same roof as their owners. This being the case, not many people would want to keep a breeding pair running around the house. Think of the smell. Think of the greasy fur rubbing against your furniture. Think of the urine marking on your carpets. Think of the male's aggressive behavior. Given these negatives, is it really practical or desirable to have a breeding pair as house pets? It's not even a good idea to keep only a female and have her bred by someone else's hob. After all, there's still the smell. In addition, there could be problems with prolonged estrus. And what if medical problems arise either with your jill or with her kits?

Are you financially prepared to deal with the veterinary bills that can mount up when mother or kits are sick? Then there's the time commitment—kits need to be socialized. They need to be handled by people on a daily basis for weeks if they're to make good pets. Breeders hire special handlers to do the job—can you make time in your busy schedule to do it yourself? And can you make time to find good homes for the kits?

The bottom line is that ferret breeding, with all its complexities and time commitments, is not an activity for the hobbyist. It's a specialized undertaking, requiring expert knowledge, that should be left to the professionals. So, if there are ferrets residing in your house, you *don't* want the stork dropping by—get your ferrets neutered or spayed.

Be sure that your ferret is neutered or spayed.

Index